Journeys in Biblical Studies:

Academic Papers from SBL International 2008, New Zealand

Hermit Kingdom Studies in History and Religion, 4

Journeys in Biblical Studies:
Academic Papers from SBL International 2008, New Zealand

Edited by

Heerak Christian Kim

The Hermit Kingdom Press
Highland Park * Seoul * Bangalore * Cebu

Journeys in Biblical Studies: Academic Papers from SBL International 2008, New Zealand
(Hermit Kingdom Studies in History and Religion, 4)

Copyright ©2008 The Hermit Kingdom Press

All rights reserved. No part of this book may be reproduced in any form or by any means, electronic or mechanical, including photocopying, recording, or by any information storage and retrieval system (including computer files in any form), without permission in writing from the publisher.

Hardcover ISBN13: 978-1-59689-146-3
Paperback ISBN13: 978-1-59689-087-9

ISSN: 1932-6696

Write To Address:
The Hermit Kingdom Press
P. O. Box 1226
Highland Park, NJ 08904-1226
The United States of America

Library of Congress Cataloging-in-Publication Data

Society of Biblical Literature. International Meeting (2008 : New Zealand)
 Journeys in biblical studies : academic papers from SBL International 2008, New Zealand / edited by Heerak Christian Kim.
   p. cm. -- (Hermit Kingdom studies in history and religion, ISSN 1932-6696 ; 4)
 Includes bibliographical references.
 ISBN 978-1-59689-146-3 (hardcover : alk. paper) -- ISBN 978-1-59689-087-9 (pbk. : alk. paper)
 1. Bible--Criticism, interpretation, etc.--Congresses. I. Kim, H. C. (Heerak Christian) II. Title.

BS511.3.S66 2008
220.6--dc22
                         2008034833

Soli Deo Gloria

Contents

Preface /Page xi/

List of Contributors /Page xv/

"Psalms of Solomon 17 as Zadokite Apocalyptic Literature: Davidic Messiah and Royal Ideology As Supporting the Displaced Zadokites"
(Heerak Christian Kim) /Page 1/

"Transgenerational Punishment in the Hebrew Bible"
(Sunwoo Hwang) /Page 20/

"Economics and Theology of Salvation In Adam Smith and Hegel"
(Yong-Sun Yang) /Page 34/

"Exodus Theme in the Book of Revelation 12-13"
(Young Mog Song) /Page 58/

"בְּבֵיתִי in 1 Chr 17:14: Temple or Kingdom?"
(Sunwoo Hwang) /Page 80/

Contents

"The Uniqueness of Jesus
As the Beauty of Harmony among Us"
(Yong-Sun Yang)   /Page 96/

"Intertextual Time Capsule of Luke 4:16-30:
The Import of Luke's Two Significant Intertextual
Additions for Understanding the Lukan Agenda"
(Heerak Christian Kim)   /Page 118/

Preface

The Protestant Christian history of Korea is a little over 100 years old. However, today, Korea sends out the most Christian missionaries, after the United States and Great Britain. Christianity has grown by leaps and bounds in Korea and with this growth came growth in interest in Biblical Studies research. Thus, it is not surprising that there are Korean researchers and scholars all over the world in the world's best academic institutions for Biblical Studies research. The Korean interest in Biblical Studies is so great that in some Christian seminaries in the United States of America, over 40% of the student body is Korean.

Ethnic Koreans have also played an important role in mainline Christian denominations in the United States. The United Methodist Church has a separate division for Korean United Methodist Church (KUMC) members, because of the strong unity, growth, and influence of Korean Methodists who have set up predominantly Korean-speaking (K)UMC churches all over America, with their formal Methodist training in UMC seminaries, like Duke University Divinity School and Northwestern University's Garrett-Evangelical Theological Seminary.

Among the mainline Presbyterians in the United States, a Korean has served as the leader ("Moderator") of the Presbyterian Church (USA) a few years ago. Since the PC (USA) is the biggest Presbyterian denomination in the United States, the fact that a Korean has led the denomination for 1 year is significant. Koreans and Korean churches are active in other Presbyterian denominations, such as the Presbyterian Church in America (PCA), which has a Korean presbytery. Since Rev. In-Ho Koh, the best friend of my father, Rev. Manwoo A. Kim, who is currently the most senior Korean Presbyterian clergy in the city of Philadelphia, has been the General Secretary of PCA for Koreans for many

Preface

years, I came to learn about the important role that Korean Christians and clergy are playing in traditionally white denominations. Koreans have become more and more active in contributing to the life and leadership of America's mainline denominations, evangelical denominations, fundamentalist Christian denominations, as well as America's leading institutes for Biblical Studies.

Ethnic Koreans are making greater and more important contributions in academic inquiry of Biblical Studies, Jewish history, history of Christianity, and religious studies. Thus, it is no surprise that more and more Koreans are presenting their important research at leading academic conferences around the world.

This important book contains a number of academic papers that were delivered at the 2008 International Meeting of the Society of Biblical Literature (SBL) in Auckland, New Zealand. As readers can see, some very important contributions to academic research into Biblical Studies is being made by ethnic Korean scholars. There are also academic articles from this volume that are from other academic conferences; they are identified in the footnote.

It is my sincere wish that the articles in this academic monograph will contribute to furthering research into Biblical Studies and also raise the profile of ethnic Koreans who are currently engaged in cutting-edge research in Biblical Studies.

The Rev. Prof. Heerak Christian Kim
Asia Evangelical College and Seminary
Bangalore, INDIA

List of Contributors

The Rev. Prof. Heerak Christian Kim is Adjunct Professor of Asia Evangelical College and Seminary in Bangalore, India. Professor Kim was the Lady Davis Fellow in the State of Israel from 1996 to 1997, and is the author of many important books, among which is *The Jerusalem Tradition in the Late Second Temple Period* (2007). He has researched at UCLA, University of Pennsylvania, Brown University, Harvard University, Cambridge University, Heidelberg University, and the Hebrew University of Jerusalem.

The Rev. Prof. Young Mog Song is Lecturer of New Testament at Kosin University in Pusan, South Korea. Prof. Song holds Th.M. from Potchefstroom University and a Doctorate in Philosophy and Literature from the University of Johannesburg in South Africa.

Professor Yong-Sun Yang teaches Systematic Theology at Wesley Institute in Sydney, Australia. Prof. Yang's journey began with an academic training in mathematics, which developed into a professional interest in economics. Gradually, interest in economics led Prof. Yang to an interest in philosophy and, finally, in theology. Prof. Yang lives in Sydney with his wife, Mi-Hea, three daughters, So-Ra, So-Ri and Ha-Neul, and one son, Jeong-Hun.

Sunwoo Hwang received his BA from Yonsei University in Seoul, South Korea. He then went to the United States, and received M.Div. from Trinity Evangelical Divinity School and S.T.M. in Old Testament from Yale University Divinity School. He then made an academic pilgrimage to Edinburgh, Scotland, and he is currently in the process of completing his Ph.D. in Hebrew and the Old Testament at the University of Edinburgh.

"Psalms of Solomon 17 as Zadokite Apocalyptic Literature: Davidic Messiah and Royal Ideology As Supporting the Displaced Zadokites"[1]

Heerak Christian Kim

The Psalms of Solomon has been touted as a messianic, or even a "Christological" text, because of the specific reference of "Anointed of the Lord" (PsSol 17:32) that guides the general flow of redemption of the Lord that is celebrated in the text, particularly in Psalms of Solomon, chapter 11. It has been debated who this apocalyptic messianic figure might be, but the scholarly consensus is that it is a messianic figure, not dissimilar to the notion of messiah contained in the New Testament.[2] In fact, Professor Marinus de Jonge of University of Leiden, the Netherlands, argues regarding the epithet in Psalms of Solomon: "The image of the 'Anointed of the Lord' and the future expectation of the 'Son of

---

[1] This academic paper was accepted by the Apocalyptic Literature section of the 2008 International Society of Biblical Literature conference in Auckland, New Zealand.

[2] It is interesting to note the current trend of Old Testament theology; there is a strong dichotomy between Christian scholars and Jewish scholars. Leo G. Purdue writes regarding what is happening on the Jewish scholarly side: "In contrast, some Jewish scholars who recently have entered in the dialogue concerning the theology of the Hebrew Bible, even if few in numbers, read and interpret the text while situated in Jewish cultures and the synagogue. However, most Jews would reject biblical theology and replace it with Jewish theology that continues this traditioning process through later corpora of texts (Mishnah, Talmud, Midrashim, Commentaries, and later Jewish thinkers)" (Leo G. Perdue, *Reconstructing Old Testament Theology: After the Collapse of History* <Minneapolis: Fortress Press, 2005>, p. 29).

David' in view of Pompey's invasion of Palestine are of great importance to the understanding of the usage of the title Messiah/Christ in the Gospels and Acts"[3]

Although Professor De Jonge has devoted a life-time to examining how terminology from the Late Second Temple period finds concurrence in the New Testament writings, I would argue that such comparisons would be enhanced by greater focus on the enhanced contextual understanding of Late Second Temple Judaism, which experienced the rise of radical apocalypticism. Thus, my focus for this article is on the reality of Psalms of Solomon as Zadokite apocalyptic literature, composed by a Zadokite during the Hasmonean period [4] to propagandize for Zadokite priesthood and Davidic kingship.[5] He, like the Zadokites

---

[3] Marinus de Jonge, *Jewish Eschatology, Early Christian Christology and the Testaments of the Twelve Patriarchs: Collected Essays* (Leiden: E. J. Brill, 1991), p. 3.

[4] One of the reasons why the Hasmonean period has been treated positively by scholars of the Second Temple period is that they were seen as heroes who saved the day for the Jews. They drove away the foreigners, purified the temple, and brought back Jewish traditions forbidden by law by a foreign power. Thus, the fact that they were traditionally not the legitimate priests to hold the office of the high priest is often ignored, intentionally or in the excitement of hero worship. Such is the case with Menahem Stern, who writes glowingly about the Hasmoneans: "The Hasmonean family, which belonged to the Watch of Jehoiarib, was held in high regard in Jewish circles and was an example and source of inspiration to the masses. For the next 130 years, the Hasmonean family was to occupy the central place in Jewish history" (Menahem Stern, "The Period of the Second Temple Period," in *A History of the Jewish People*, ed. H. H. Ben-Sasson <Cambridge: Harvard University Press, 1976, pp. 185-303>, p. 206).

[5] Solomon Zeitlin argues that Hasmoneans intentionally overthrew the Zadokites in an armed revolt. Zeitlin writes: "Hence what began primarily as a resistance movement against the religious persecutions of Antiochus IV must also be seen as a revolt against the Zadokite high priests. This helps explain one result of the victory. Despite Pentateuchal law, the Zadokite dynasty was overthrown, theocracy was abolished and a high priest not of the Zadokite family was elected by the people" (Solomon Zeitlin, *The Rise and Fall of the Judaean State: A Political, Social and Religious History of the Second Commonwealth (Volume One 332-37 B.C.E.)* <Philadelphia: The Jewish Publication Society of America, 1962>, pp. 176-177). It is important to note, however, that people's support for

in Qumran and elsewhere, were interested in reinstating the Zadokite high priesthood, which was tied to a Davidic king. It was the Zadokite struggle for reinstatement that prompted the author's apocalyptic tone and aggressive apologizing for a David monarch.[6] For the author, it was not an abstraction or a mere literary exercise; rather, it represented the life-and-death struggle of Zadokites, who were being pursued by the Wicked Priest and the ruling Hasmonean faction.[7] Understanding the Zadokite struggle helps

---

the Hasmoneans was due to Maccabean military victory, not dissimilar to initial support of US President Bush after Iraq victory.

[6] King David was the key, not only because it was a Davidide who instituted Zadokites as legitimate High Priests of Israel, but also because it was King David who conquered Jerusalem and made it the seat of the cultic worship of Yahweh with his son building the Temple. Furthermore, reforms, such as by Josiah, focused on the centrality of the Jerusalem cult in the "City of David" (J. Alberto Soggin, *A History of Ancient Israel*, trans. John Bowden <Philadelphia: The Westminster Press, 1984>, p. 245).

[7] Morton Smith writes: "In the middle of the second century, when the legitimate representative of the Jerusalem high priesthood was deprived of his position, he went to Leontopolis in Egypt and built a temple there. So the cult of Yahweh was disseminated from a number of centers known to us – Haran, Elephantine, Babylonia, Lachish, Samaria, Gerizim, Tabor, Carmel, Hermon, Hebron and Mamre, Deir 'Alla, Tell es-sa-'idiyeh, 'Araq el-Emir, Leontopolis – and probably from others of which we have no record. (Consequently, postexilic 'Israel' cannot be equated with the adherents of the Jerusalem temple. The term was claimed also by other worshippers of Yahweh, both those who had other temples and those who had none.)" (Morton Smith, *Palestinian Parties and Politics That Shaped the Old Testament* <New York: Columbia University Press, 1971>, pp. 92-93). The fact that expelled (or fugitive) Zadokites were able to set up Jewish Temple and holy places goes back to the experience of Jews in the Exile and in the Diaspora. William Horbury writes: "Despite the primacy of the land of Israel and the Jerusalem sanctuary, the 'holy land' and the 'holy hill' (Zech. 2.12; 8.3; Wis. 9.8; 12.3), both at home and abroad there were other places which in practice acquired an aura of sanctity. .... Wherever Jews settled, therefore, some spots were sanctified by assembly and building or by remembrance of Israel's settlement, salvation and human leadership; but this network of places only emphasized the holiness of the specifically chosen land and sanctuary" (William Horbury, "Land, Sanctuary and Worship" in *Early Christian Thought in Its Jewish Context*, eds. John Barclay and John Sweet <Cambridge: Cambridge University Press, 1996, pp. 207-224>, pp. 213-214).

the understanding of how the concept of a Davidic messiah was kept alive in a period, leading to the writing of the New Testament.[8]

The epithet, "Anointed of the Lord," found in Psalms of Solomon 17:32, can be seen as a key signifier[9] employed by the composer of the Psalms of Solomon to trigger[10] the collective memory[11] of King David as the legitimate king[12] over Israel and all

---

[8] Unfortunately, many biblical studies scholars tended to homogenize Judaism and assume their relative unity. But this is not true. There were violent factions within Judaism. Wrong assumption of unified Judaism is found in E. Earle Ellis' statement: "In its interpretation of Scripture the community of Jesus is rooted in and remains in continuity with the larger community of religious Judaism. It follows exegetical methods very similar to other groups and is distinguished primarily in the emphasis given to some procedures and in the boldness with which they were applied. In its general conceptual frame of reference it is closest to apocalyptic Judaism and thus, in some respects, to the Qumran community, but here also it is not without affinities with the Pharisaic-rabbinic and Sadducean parties" (E. Earle Ellis, *The Old Testament in Early Christianity: Canon and Interpretation in the Light of Modern Research* <Tübingen: J. C. B. Mohr (Paul Siebeck), 1991>, p. 77). Ellis is not alone; in fact, majority of scholars in the field tend to homogenize Judaism. In my paper, I place in diametric opposition Zadokite priests and Hasmonean priests who kicked them out of Jerusalem. Qumran is a part of Zadokite priestly community in flight/exile.

[9] See Heerak Christian Kim, *Key Signifier as Literary Device: Its Definition and Function in Literature and Media* (Lewiston: The Edwin Mellen Press, 2006).

[10] The Exile prompted emphasis on the ideals of tradition. This was the case with Ezekiel. H. G. M. Williamson writes: "Whether the distance of exile affected his outlook or not, he broke completely with prevailing reality in order to initiate (or return to) an idealistic, even utopian, view of Israel..." (H. G. M. Williamson, "The Concept of Israel in Transition," in *The World of Ancient Israel: Sociological, Anthropological and Political Perspectives*, ed. R. E. Clements <Cambridge: Cambridge University Press, 1989, pp. 141-161>. Of course, this includes royal ideology of the eternal throne of David the King.

[11] Collective memory can be seen as "collective mind." Raphael Patai describes the Jewish mind as "a product of Jewish culture, and Jewish culture as a product of the Jewish mind. Jewish religion – unquestionably the most important element in Jewish culture – is likewise considered as a product of the Jewish mind. We shall see how this collective mind reacted to the incessant flow of outside cultural influences to which the Jews were exposed throughout their

the David royal ideology¹³ attached to that traditional value. Strongly attached to Davidic royal ideology is the idea that the Zadokites, the descendants of Zadok the High Priest appointed by the Davidic King Solomon for the Jerusalem Temple¹⁴ he built, are

---

history" (Raphael Patai, *The Jewish Mind* <Detroit: Wayne State University Press, 1977>, p. 3). Patai further writes: "For this reason it is evidently not possible to discuss the Jewish mind without constant reference to the Gentile environment whose impact so greatly contributed to its formation" (Patai, p. 5).

¹² Christopher R. Seitz writes: "The biblical texts themselves also clarify the distinctiveness of dynastic kingship in the south as deriving from Yahweh's special choice of David (2 Sam 7:13-16; 1 Kgs 9:5). This fact ought not be underestimated, since it contributed to whatever stability Judah experienced during the period under discussion" (Christopher R. Seitz, *Theology in Conflict: Reactions to the Exile in the Book of Jeremiah* <Berlin: Walter de Gruyter, 1989>, p. 21).

¹³ One of the reasons why Davidic royal ideology was emphasized and enmeshed in popular collective memory is that King Solomon used it to legitimize his rule. Tomoo Ishida writes: "Under these circumstances, the regime of Solomon had to lay emphasis first on the continuity of the dynasty, since the throne of David was the sole foundation of his kingship when it was established" (Tomoo Ishida, *History and Historical Writing in Ancient Israel: Studies in Biblical Historiography* <Leiden: Brill, 1999>, p. 123).

¹⁴ One of the reasons for the strength of the tradition was that Zadok became the first High Priest of the Jerusalem Temple in the midst of radical cultic centralization effort of King Solomon. Martin Sicker writes: "Solomon's surprising order of priority may have been a deliberate gesture to Zadok, a reward for his support. It is also noteworthy, in this regard, that Solomon basically agreed with Abiathar that Jerusalem should be the principle cultic center; however, Solomon soon demoted Abiathar and brought Zadok from the sanctuary at Gibeon to Jerusalem to become the sole high priest" (Martin Sicker, *The Rise and Fall of the Ancient Israelite State* <Westport: Praeger, 2003>, p. 163). Max L. Margolis and Alexander Marx write: "In their stead Solomon appointed the sons of Zadok, the priest who favored his own accession; these sons of Zadok remained in office until the Maccabees stepped into their place. In the temple of Onias in Egypt the Zadokites continued until the closing of their sanctuary by the Romans (Max L. Margolis and Alexander Marx, *A History of the Jewish People* <Fairfield: A Temple Book, 1985>, p. 64). The temple of Onias was the Jewish temple in Leontopolis, Egypt. The Leontopolis temple was destroyed after the destruction of the Jerusalem Temple in 70 AD.

the legitimate priestly authorities[15] from whom the post of the High Priest should be filled.[16] The composer of the Psalms of Solomon, who is a Zadokite himself, intended to effectuate the second triggering afterwards of causing the readers of Psalms of Solomon to rally behind the Zadokites against the Hasmoneans,[17] illegitimate priests who had usurped both the legitimate priestly positions from the Zadokites and the royal authority from the Davidic line. Psalms of Solomon 17, the chapter in which the key signifier is found, can, in fact, be seen as a Zadokite propaganda treatise to prove this point.

Psalms of Solomon 17 can be seen as a treatise on why King David is legitimate and should rule in Israel and what happens when his legitimacy is undermined. This is clearly

---

[15] The Zadokite priestly legitimacy was recognized during and after the Exile. Roland de Vaux writes regarding the return from the Babylonian Exile: "We have seen that the first caravans to return included priests who were probably Sadoqites, and the evidence given in the Book of Esdras, Aggaeus and Zacharias about the restoration of worship in Jerusalem contains no trace of any opposition from a non-Sadoqite group which was already in possession of the Temple" (Roland de Vaux, *Ancient Israel: Its Life and Institutions*, trans. John McHugh <Grand Rapids: William B. Eerdmans Publishing Company, 1997>, p. 396).

[16] Roland de Vaux writes: "Sadoq was a descendant of Eleazar and Ebyathar a descendant of Ithamar. David divided the work between the two families by instituting twenty-four classes of priests.... Thenceforward all the priests could be called 'sons of Aaron,' but the Sadoqites still retained a certain distinction: their ancestor Eleazar is presented as more noble than Ithamar.... Finally, they [Zadokites] continued to provide the high priest down to the time of Antiochus Epiphanes (De Vaux, p. 397).

[17] Martin Noth notes that the Hasmoneans had a tenuous support base in Palestine and lacked real legitimacy. Noth writes: "For this monarchy lacked a really firm basis. David's monarchy had been sustained by the consent of the free Israelite tribes in the two kingdoms of Judah and Israel, whereas, to begin with, the Hasmonean monarchy relied very largely on the support of a particular party in the little province of Judah; and even though it did reach out quite far beyond these narrow confines, the make-up of the people on which it must base itself had become far too disunited after centuries of foreign rule and many vicissitudes of fate to form the basis of a permanent political structure" (Martin Noth, *The History of Israel* <New York: Harper & Row, Publishers, 1960>, p. 385).

evident in the historical block within the chapter, found in verses five to twenty-two. First of all, the historical section begins with King David, rather than Abraham, Adam, or Moses. This is strategic and not accidental.[18] The composer of the Psalms of Solomon wanted to emphasize Davidic royal ideology, so that he starts his historical recounting of Israel's history from King David. Psalms of Solomon 17:5 proclaims: "You, O LORD, chose David king over Israel, and you swore to him regarding his seed into eternity, that his kingdom would not fall before you." The composer of the Psalms of Solomon ignores the fact of God's covenant-making with Abraham. It was as if God's relationship with Israel started with King David and God's promise to his royal line. This testifies to the fact that the composer was a Zadokite, who was interested in asserting the legitimacy of Zadokite high priesthood. Since it was the Davidic line that appointed Zadokites as high priests of the Jerusalem Temple, the restoration of the Davidic kingship and its continuance would ensure Zadokite high priesthood. Since the days of King Solomon, the Zadokite high priesthood has been closely associated with Davidic kingship, which legitimized its position in the Jerusalem Temple. Had the composer of Psalms of Solomon started with Abraham as the starting point of his mini-history of Israel, that would have detracted from his propagandistic goal to support the Zadokites and oppose the Hasmoneans. Hasmoneans, like the Zadokites,

---

[18] In a sense, the author of the Psalms of Solomon was concerned not with Diaspora Jews, but with the local politics of Jerusalem, from where the legitimate Zadokites was dispelled. In other words, the poet focused on Jerusalem Jews and not diaspora Jews, who lived within Diapora politics. Erich S. Gruen describes Diaspora Jews' separatedness from Jerusalem: "But a comparable dilemma did not face the Jews who dwelled in Greco-Roman communities in the Second Temple period. Jerusalem (for most of that time) stood under Jewish rule, welcoming to pilgrims, visitors, or repatriates. The Jews abroad had chosen their residence voluntarily and (in many cases) had been there for generations. They had no cause to ache for Jerusalem. Nor, by contrast, were they obliged to adopt a new guise and sacrifice their identity to blend in with their surroundings" (Erich S. Gruen, *Diaspora: Jews amidst Greeks and Romans* <Cambridge: Harvard University Press, 2002>, p. 5).

were Jews who claimed to be children of the covenant and legitimate partakers of the covenantal blessings. Starting with Abraham would minimize the Zadokite author's intention to attack the Hasmoneans for usurping the high priesthood and the throne of Israel.

    Furthermore, the Zadokite author of the Psalms of Solomon did not start his mini-history with Moses or the Exodus for the same reason that he wrote the Psalms of Solomon as a propaganda literature against Hasmoneans and for the Zadokites. Hasmoneans, just like the Zadokites, were beneficiaries of the deliverance by God in the Exodus. They could claim to be descendants of those who participated in the receiving of the Ten Commandments and the Laws of God to Moses. More importantly, the Mosaic Law does not require that a Zadokite be the high priest. A high priest could come from the tribe of Levi. The Hasmoneans, just like the Zadokites, met the minimum requirement under the Mosaic Law to occupy the position of the high priest of the Jerusalem Temple. Thus, starting the mini-history with Moses in Psalms of Solomon 17 would have detracted from the Zadokite author's intention to attack the Hasmoneans as illegitimate and to legitimize the Zadokites for the office of the high priest. Thus, the Zadokite composer went to the original source for legitimizing the Zadokite high priesthood; namely, Davidic Royal Ideology. It was the Davidic royal line that appointed Zadok as the high priest of the Jerusalem Temple. And the tradition of appointing descendants of Zadok was perpetuated and maintained under Davidic kings. Davidic royal ideology, therefore, was the legitimizing source for Zadokite high priesthood, not the Abrahamic covenant or the Mosaic Law.

    The fact that King David is the starting point for the author's mini-history also provides evidence that the author was not a Pharisee, as Ryle and James have assumed and argued in their monumental commentary on the Psalms of Solomon, published about a century ago. If the author of the Psalms of Solomon were Pharisees, they would not have missed the opportunity to start the mini-history of Israel with Moses or the

Exodus. For the Pharisees, the Law of Moses was of prime importance. For them, the history of Israel essentially started with the Mosaic Law. The Pharisees were strong adherents to the Mosaic Law and called on the authority of Moses on every point of Jewish religious practice and faith. The fact that the author of the Psalms of Solomon does not emphasis Moses or the Mosaic Law militates against the scholarly consensus that the Psalms of Solomon was written by a Pharisee.

The author of the Psalms of Solomon was a Zadokite, who was resolved to push his pro-Zadokite propaganda. The content of mini-history found in Psalms of Solomon 17:5-22 further affirms this. The mini-history shows that the David royal line was not to be blamed for the evils that befell on Israel.[19] Psalms of Solomon 17:6 argues: "And the sinners rose up against us in our sins; they overtook us and expelled us. You did not promise to them; they took with violence." It is clear that Psalms of Solomon 17:6 is referring to the Babylonian Exile since the phrase, "they overtook us and expelled us." Of course, "they" refer to the Babylonians.

---

[19] Jon D. Levenson writes: "For the fact is that the psalm [89], like Nathan's oracle, states distinctly that God will uphold David's posterity at all cost, even – and here the contrast with Sinai could not be sharper – if they break the commandments and desecrate divine law" (Jon D. Levenson, *Sinai & Zion: An Entry into the Jewish Bible* <San Francisco: Harper & Row, Publishers, 1985>, p. 99). Levenson distinguishes God's covenant with David from God's covenant at Sinai; Israelites were required to keep their part of the law, but David did not have such an obligation. Levenson writes: "This Davidic covenant, then, is distinct in kind from the Sinaitic. The focus of the Mosaic covenant sealed at Sinai is twofold: history and morality. God there formalizes a longstanding relationship and benevolence (on his part, at least) into a pact through which Israel might reflect back to God some of the grace she has known. The historical prologue establishes the claim upon Israel which the latter discharges only through observance of the *mitsvot*. The dynamics of Sinai, which are the dynamics of the treaty, metamorphose history into morality, or in rabbinic language, *aggadah* into *halakah*, lore into law" (Levenson 100). Also, see Noth, *The History of Israel*, p. 289. This can be described as prophetic and Deuteronomistic view of the Old Testament (J. Maxwell Miller and John H. Hayes, *A History of Ancient Israel and Judah* <Philadelphia: The Westminster Press, 1986>, p. 421).

Furthermore, it is clear that they were Gentiles because of the stated idea that those who kicked them out of Israel and took away the Jerusalem Temple were people who did not receive any promise from God. And Psalms of Solomon 17:15 describes the foreign ruler who led the destruction: "And his heart was alien from our God." But the Zadokite author is clear who should be blamed for the Babylonian Exile. The culprits for the Babylonian Exile were "we." Of course, the Zadokite composer is trying to place the blame for God's judgment on the people,[20] rather than on Davidic kings. This is not surprising given the fact that the Zadokite composer is writing a propaganda literature for the Zadokites and the Davidic royal line which legitimated its high priesthood. People were at fault and not the Davidic king, whom God has chosen.

This is different from the biblical position that the corruption of the Davidic line, such as Solomon intermarrying foreign women and bringing idolatry in, was at least partly to blame for the fall of Israel. But any hint of this would not help the Zadokite author's intention to create a propaganda literature for the Zadokites. If the Davidic line fell into some sin, could not the high priests appointed by the Davidic line be blamed as well for the moral failings of the royal line which appointed it and perpetuated its legitimacy? The fault for the Babylonian Exile did not belong to the Davidic kings or to Zadokite priests, but rather, it belonged to the people who sinned. Psalms of Solomon 17:17 describes that the children of the covenant surpassed the Gentiles in doing evil.

---

[20] Susan Niditch writes: "Finally the kingdoms are conquered, the North by the superpower Assyria, the Southern Davidic kingdom by Babylonia, events regarded as punishment for Israel's sin" (Susan Niditch, *Ancient Israelite Religion* <New York: Oxford University Press, 1997>, p. 8). Frederic W. Bush emphasizes that the covenant itself required Israelite obedience. Bush writes: "thus, the Mosaic covenant of obligation held over the heads of the people of God a desperately serious threat: if they failed to keep the covenant stipulations, terrible judgment – even utter destruction – would fall upon them" (Frederic W. Bush, "Images of Israel: The People of God in the Torah," *Studies in Old Testament Theology*, eds. Robert L. Hubbard, Jr., Robert K. Johnston, and Robert P. Meye <Dallas: Word Publishing, 1992, pp. 99-115>, p. 104).

Furthermore, Psalms of Solomon 17:17 specifically points out two transgressions; namely, not pursuing mercy and truth. This can be seen as an allusion to the way Zadokites were pushed out by the Hasmoneans from their legitimate positions in the Jerusalem Temple and hunted down like dogs. There was no mercy. And the truth that the Zadokites should be the high priests and that the royal throne should be occupied by a Davidic king was pushed aside.

The Zadokite composer of the Psalms of Solomon continues his pro-Zadokite mini-history of Israel by describing that God destroyed the Gentile power that destroyed the Davidic kingdom. Psalms of Solomon 17:8 is emphatic in showing God's judgment for the destruction of Davidic kingdom, and not for the slaughter of the populace in Jerusalem. In fact, Psalms of Solomon 17:13-14 is emphatic in the point that it was God's judgment for the Jews in Jerusalem to be annihilated and sent into the Exile. God was punishing the people for their sins. Psalms of Solomon 17:26 encapsulates Gods judgmental destruction of sinning Jews: "May he expel the sinners from the inheritance; may he annihilate the pride of the sinners; may he break in pieces their substance like the potter's vessels with an iron rod!" In the context of the Zadokite author's writing, it is understandable why he emphasized God's judgmental killing of fellow Jews. The Hasmoneans, who were Jews, pushed Zadokites out of their legitimate positions in the Jerusalem Temple. It was the Jewish people who went along with the Hamonean program against the Zadokites. For the Zadokite composer of the Psalms of Solomon, it was only justice that God was killing the fellow Jews who stood by as Zadokites were exiled and hunted down. The Zadokite composer of the Psalms of Solomon's propaganda involved triggering the collective memory of God's judgement in the Babylonian Exile as a threat to his contemporary Jews for not practicing mercy toward Zadokite priests and for not remembering the truth of God's demands for the Jerusalem Temple.[21] The Zadokites should be empowered at the

---

[21] The attitude of the composer of the Psalms of Solomon was in line with the tone of Old Testament worldview. Walter Brueggemann writes: "Israel now knows, with the memory available and the liturgy ringing in its ear, that public

Jerusalem Temple and not the Hasmoneans. The people were "sinning" by allowing the Hasmoneans to mistreat the Zadokites. And just as God annihilated Jews for their "sins," God can kill Jews of today for their "sins." The Zadokite propaganda is clear.

In the context of Psalms of Solomon 17, there is a picture into the state of the Zadokites at the time of the composition of the poems. Many Zadokites left corrupt Jerusalem for the desert. Psalms of Solomon 17:18-19 states: "Those who love the gathering of the saints fled from them, like sparrows scattering from their nest. They wandered in desert places, to preserve their souls from evil, and precious in the eyes of the sojourning was a soul saved from them." Zadokites were forced into the desert by the Hasmoneans who were hunting them down and trying to secure their power in Jerusalem. Zadokites were the primary threats to the Hasmoneans because they were legitimate priests. Psalms of Solomon 17:18-19 account of Zadokites fleeing to the desert corresponds to the historical community of Qumran and the testimonials of Teacher of Righteousness. The Wicked Priest in Jerusalem was trying to hunt down the Teacher of Righteousness. Zadokites were in a struggle for their lives because of the illegitimate priests who were occupying power positions in Jerusalem.[22] This portion of the composition was a reminder to the

---

power cannot be arranged for stratification, exploitation, and oppression. Such social order is a disorder that will generate more cries to Yahweh against the status quo, and such cries will provoke Yahweh into decisive transformative activity. A cry of oppression will mobilize this hearing God against any agents of hurt (cf. Exod. 22:21-27). Israel's public power and its institutional forms must be ordered to eliminate the cause of such voiced hurt" (Walter Brueggemann, *Old Testament Theology: Essays on Structure, Theme, and Text*, ed. Patrick D. Miller <Minneapolis: Fortress Press, 1992>, p. 49).

[22] It is important to note that Zadokites were a real threat to Hasmoneans because of the perception that the High Priest was not only a religious leader, but a political leader as well. Menachem Stern writes: "If the Hasmoneans had relinquished the High Priesthood and allowed it to fall into other hands, their political power would have been undermined and their other offices deprived of all real substance, for the people had grown accustomed to regard the High Priest as their supreme leader. Domestically also the office of the High Priest ranked above the other functions of the Hasmonean rulers; it is this title that was

Zadokite author's readers of the current situation of the Zadokites and what was wrong with Israel.

What would be right is if the Davidic king could be restored to the throne of Israel.[23] The Zadokite author of the Psalms of Solomon states: "Look, O LORD, and lift up for them their king, a son of David, into the time you know, O God, to rule over Israel, your slave, and gird him with strength to cast down unjust rulers!" (PsSol 17:23-24). These two verses function to show the readers that there is something seriously wrong in Israel. A Davidic king does not sit on the throne of Israel, but rather a Hasmonean.[24] God will correct the horrible wrong situation by bringing a Davidic king who will save Israel from the illegitimate Hasmonean dynasty. Of course, a reminder of the illegitimacy of Hasmonean kingship is a reminder of the illegitimacy of the Hasmonean high priesthood. Just as it is only right that a descendant of David be king over Israel, it is only right that a descendant of Zadok be the high priest in Jerusalem. An argument for the legitimacy of a Davidic king is necessarily an argument for the legitimacy of a Zadokite high priest.

So, why is the Zadokite poet-composer of the Psalms of Solomon not more explicit in his push for bringing back the

---

usually stressed in the Hebrew inscriptions on the coins struck by them, including the last of the dynasty" (Menachem Stern, "The Period of the Second Temple," in *A History of the Jewish People*, ed. H. H. Ben-Sasson, p. 229). The Hasmoneans were aware that people perceived that the throne should be occupied by a descendant of David. But as rededicators of the Jerusalem Temple, the Hasmoneans felt that they had acquired the legitimacy in popular perception to be High Priest of the Jerusalem Temple.

[23] Leonhard Rost argues that God's promise that David's kingdom will last forever, found in the prophecy of Nathan in 2 Samuel 7 can be dated to the earliest strata, to the time of David himself (Leonhard Rost, *The Succession to the Throne of David* <Sheffield: The Almond Press, 1989>, pp. 45-48).

[24] John M. Oesterreicher describes longing for King David as an expression of discontent about current kings. Oesterreicher writes: "There was no end to the longing for newness. Disappointed by her many kings – caricatures rather than real servants of God and of the people – Israel yearned for a return of the days of David" (John M. Oesterreicher, *The Israel of God: On the Old Testament Roots of the Church's Faith* <Englewood Cliffs: Prentice-Hall, Inc., 1963>, pp. 80-81).

Zadokites and pushing out the Hasmoneans? The answer is found in the socio-political environment in which the composer finds himself. The Hasmoneans have firmly entrenched themselves in power positions in Israel, both religious and political. There was a Hasmonean on the royal throne, and there was a Hasmonean in the office of the high priest at the Jerusalem Temple. Many enforcers of laws in Israel and lesser dignitaries were Hasmonean or pro-Hasmonean. Those who were pro-Zadokite were endangered, so they found themselves having to communicate in a less explicit manner. The Psalms of Solomon represents a composition by a Zadokite who wanted to use it as propaganda for Zadokites, but he could not do so openly or explicitly because he could be subject to persecution by Hasmoneans and their supporters. Thus, he found a literary channel that would allow him to push Zadokite propaganda that would not incriminate himself. Thus, the whole composition of the Psalms of Solomon seem "sanitary" in that it describes what seems to be generic themes of value to the Jews of his time, such as keeping the law, remembering the judgement of God in the exile, and emphasizing devotion to God. But the Zadokite poet-composer tackles traditional themes in an artful manner, using the literary device of the key signifier. The key signifier is "Anointed of the Lord" which triggers the collective memory of the Jews of his time who are to remember that Davidic king is the legitimately anointed king over Israel and his throne is not supposed to have an end, by Gentiles or by Jews like the Hasmoneans. Since the Zadokites were legitimate high priests under Davidic kings, the key signifier of "Anointed of the Lord "necessarily triggers the collective memory of the readers that the Zadokites were legitimate high priests and not the Hasmoneans. In a time of political peril and real threat to their lives, Zadokites found ways to push pro-Zadokite propaganda through the genre of apocalyptic literature. The Psalms of Solomon is one example of a skilful apocalyptic literature, pushing propaganda on behalf of the Zadokites. In its couched form, the Zadokite author could make his composition available to all Jews without incriminating himself. In short, the Psalms of Solomon is a masterful propaganda literature of the Zadokites that stands as a paragon of what a skilful apocalyptic literature with a propaganda purpose on behalf of the oppressed was at a time when their life was under threat by those who have wrongfully, albeit cleverly, seized reigns of power.

Bibliography

Atkinson, Kenneth. *I Cried to the Lord: A Study of the Psalms of Solomon's Historical Background and Social Setting.* Leiden: Brill, 2004.

Atkinson, Kenneth. *An Intertextual Study of the Psalms of Solomon Pseudepigrapha.* Lewiston: The Edwin Mellon Press, 2001.

Barclay, John, and John Sweet (Editors). *Early Christian Thought in its Jewish Context.* Cambridge: Cambridge University Press, 1996.

Ben-Sasson, H. H. (Editor). *A History of the Jewish People.* Cambridge: Harvard University Press, 1976.

Brueggemann, Walter. *Old Testament Theology: Essays on Structure, Theme, and Text.* Edited by Patrick D. Miller. Minneapolis: Fortress Press, 1992.

Clements, R. E. *The World of Ancient Israel: Sociological, Anthropological and Political Perspectives.* Cambridge: Cambridge University Press, 1989.

De Jonge, Marinus. *Jewish Eschatology, Early Christian Christology and the Testaments of the Twelve Patriarchs: Collected Essays.* Leiden: E. J. Brill, 1991.

De Vaux, Roland. *Ancient Israel: Its Life and Institutions.* Translated by John McHugh. Grand Rapids: William B. Eerdmans Publishing Company, 1997.

Ellis, E. Earle. *The Old Testament in Early Christianity: Canon and Interpretation in the Light of Modern Research.* Tübingen: J. C. B. Mohr (Paul Siebeck), 1991.

Frakenberg, W. *Die Datierung der Psalmen Salomos: Ein Beitrage zur jüdischen Geschichte.* Giessen: J. Ricker, 1896.

Gera, Dor. *Judaea and Mediterranean Politics 219 to 161 B.C.E.* Leiden: Brill, 1998.

Gruen, Erich S. *Diaspora: Jews amidst Greeks and Romans.* Cambridge: Harvard University Press, 2002.

Hubbard, Robert L., Jr., Robert K. Johnston, and Robert P. Meye (Editors). *Studies in Old Testament Theology.* Dallas: Word Publishing, 1992.

Ishida, Tomoo. *History and Historical Writing in Ancient Israel: Studies in Biblical Historiography.* Leiden: Brill, 1999.

Koehler, Ludwig. *Old Testament Theology.* Translated by A. S. Todd. London: Lutterworth Press, 1957.

Kim, Heerak Christian. *Key Signifier as Literary Device: Its Definition and Function in Literature and Media.* Lewiston: The Edwin Mellen Press, 2006.

Kim, Heerak Christian. *Psalms of Solomon: A New Translation and Introduction.* Highland Park: The Hermit Kingdom Press, 2008.

Kim, Heerak Christian. *The Jerusalem Tradition in the Late Second Temple Period: Diachronic and Synchronic Developments Surrounding Psalms of Solomon 11.* Lanham: University Press of America, 2007.

Levenson, Jon D. *Sinai & Zion: An Entry into the Jewish Bible.* San Francisco: Harper & Row, Publishers, 1985.

Mansoor, Menahem. *Jewish History and Thought: An Introduction.* Hoboken: Ktav Publishing House, Inc., 1991.

Margolis, Max L., and Alexander Marx. *A History of the Jewish People.* Fairfield: A Temple Book, 1985.

Matthews, Victor H., and Don C. Benjamin. *Social World of Ancient Israel 1250-587 BCE.* Peabody: Hendrickson Publishers, Inc., 1993.

Miller, J. Maxwell, and John H. Hayes. *A History of Ancient Israel and Judah.* Philadelphia: The Westminster Press, 1986.

Movers, F. K. "Apokryphen-Literature," in *Kirchen-Lexikon, oder Encyklopädie der katholischen Theologie und ihrer Hilfswissenschaften (1).* Edited by H. J. Wetzer and B. Welte. Freiburg im Breisgau: Herder, 1947.

Niditch, Susan. *Ancient Israelite Religion.* New York: Oxford University Press, 1997.

Noth, Martin. *The History of Israel.* New York: Harper & Row, Publishers, 1960.

Oesterreicher, John M. *The Israel of God: On the Old Testament Roots of the Church's Faith.* Englewood Cliffs: Prentice-Hall, Inc., 1963.

Patai, Raphael. *The Jewish Mind.* Detroit: Wayne State University Press, 1997.

Perdue, Leo G. *Reconstructing Old Testament Theology: After the Collapse of History*. Minneapolis: Fortress Press, 2005.

Rost, Leonhard. *The Succession to the Throne of David*. Sheffield: The Almond Press, 1982.

Seitz, Christopher R. *Theology in Conflict: Reactions to the Exilic in the Book of Jeremiah*. Berlin: Walter de Gruyter, 1989.

Sicker, Martin. *The Rise and Fall of the Ancient Israelite States*. Westport: Praeger, 2003.

Smith, Morton. *Palestinian Parties and Politics that Shaped the Old Testament*. New York: Columbia University Press, 1971.

Soggin, J. Alberto. *A History of Ancient Israel*. Translated by John Bowden. Philadelphia: The Westminster Press, 1984.

Zeitlin, Solomon. *The Rise and Fall of the Judaean State: A Political, Social and Religious History of the Second Commonwealth (Volume One 332-37 B.C.E.)*. Philadelphia: The Jewish Publication Society of America, 1962.

"Transgenerational Punishment in the Hebrew Bible"[1]

Sunwoo Hwang

Introduction

What does the Hebrew Bible teach about transgenerational punishment? It is not a simple question to answer, since there seem to be two different positions in the Hebrew Bible. The clearest example of the comparison between the two positions can be made by noticing the sharp difference between the second commandment of the Decalogue (Exod 20:5) and Ezekiel's polemic against retribution to descendants (Ezek 18:4):

> You shall not bow down to them or worship them; for I, the LORD your God, am a jealous God, punishing children for the iniquity of parents, to the third and the fourth generation of those who reject me. (Exod 20:5, NRSV)

> Know that all lives are mine; the life of the parent as well as the life of the child is mine: it is only the person who sins that shall die. (Ezek 18:4, NRSV)

The problem of the two different positions was noticed very early by rabbis in Mishnaic and Talmudic times, and they made manifold attempts to solve the problem.[2] Julius Wellhausen

---

[1] This academic paper was accepted by the Concept Analysis and the Hebrew Bible section of the 2008 International Society of Biblical Literature conference in Auckland, New Zealand.

[2] See Reinhard Neudecker, "Does God visit the iniquity of the fathers upon their children?," *Gregorianum* 81 (2000), 5-23.

viewed the two distinct principles as consecutive elements in his evolutionary scheme of history of Israelite religion. While most recent scholars consider the two principles as concurrent concepts, the independence of individuality was more supported from the exilic period.[3] Concerning this highly debated issue, I will investigate biblical passages which include differing views on retribution and seek the most appropriate way of understanding the two seemingly contradictory positions in the Canon of the Hebrew Bible. Taken from what I judge to be the earliest to latest traditions, the eight passages relevant to retribution which I will analyze are[4]: Exod 34:7; Num 14:18; Exod 20:5-6 (Deut 5:9-10); Deut 24:16; Lev 26:39; Jer 31:29-30; Lam 5:7 and Ezek 18:2-4.

Interpretation of Transgenerational Retribution Passages

1. Exod 34:7

נֹצֵר חֶסֶד לָאֲלָפִים נֹשֵׂא עָוֹן וָפֶשַׁע וְחַטָּאָה
וְנַקֵּה לֹא יְנַקֶּה פֹּקֵד עֲוֹן אָבוֹת עַל־בָּנִים
וְעַל־בְּנֵי בָנִים עַל־שִׁלֵּשִׁים וְעַל־רִבֵּעִים׃

Keeping steadfast love for the thousands, forgiving iniquity and transgression and sin, yet by no means clearing the guilty, but visiting the iniquity of the parents upon the children and the children's children, to the third and the fourth generation. (My translation)

---

[3] Joze Krasovec, "Is There a doctrine of Collective Retribution in the Hebrew Bible?," *Hebrew Union College Annual* 65 (2001), 86.
[4] I will provide the rationale for my analysis as I progress in the exegesis of the passages.

This statement is made in the context of Israel's rebellion to God by making the golden calf and God's restoration of Israel by remaking the covenant. The Lord is merciful God who keeps חֶסֶד and gives a second chance to Israel; who made apostasy to the golden calf. Grammatically, the meaning of אֲלָפִים can be either "thousands," with an unrestricted sense, or "thousandth," as in generations. The RSV and the NIV follow the first option, while the NRSV and the NAB agree with the second option. Between the two options, exegetically, "thousands" is more plausible when we consider the content of the verse as a whole. If we take the second option, "thousandth" generation, it is difficult to explain why the sins of the following generations, up to the fourth, are not included in God's חֶסֶד. If we agree with the first option, the flow of this verse is smooth. God's loving-kindness is for the thousands, but the guilt shall not be removed without paying for it. It will be visited upon subsequent generations, up to the fourth.

At first glance, לְאֶלֶף דּוֹר in Deut 7:9 seems to provides a clue in favor of the second option.

וְיָדַעְתָּ כִּי־יְהוָה אֱלֹהֶיךָ הוּא הָאֱלֹהִים הָאֵל
הַנֶּאֱמָן שֹׁמֵר הַבְּרִית וְהַחֶסֶד לְאֹהֲבָיו וּלְשֹׁמְרֵי
מִצְוֹתוֹ לְאֶלֶף דּוֹר:

> Know therefore that the LORD your God is God, the faithful God who maintains covenant loyalty with those who love him and keep his commandments, to a **thousand generations**. (My emphasis added, NRSV)

However, if we read the text closely the two texts do not deal with same subject. God's loving-kindness in Exod 34:7 is for the sinners who made apostasy to the golden calf, while God's loving-kindness for thousand generations in Deut 7:9 is for those who love Him and keep His commandments.

"Transgenerational Punishment in the Hebrew Bible"

Exod 34:7 has an intriguing principle of God's mercy. God is merciful for those who committed sins, but God seems to be unfair to the following generations who take the sins of their ancestors. How do we understand divine justice in this passage? Interestingly, this principle is cited to show God's loving-kindness. God's loving-kindness lies in the deferral of punishment. As Levin Baruch points out, "we cannot therefore interpret the delaying punishment stated in the pronouncement of the attributes as an injustice, and must regard deferral as essentially an act of divine kindness."[5] The examples of deferral of God's punishment as His loving-kindness are seen in the several places of the Hebrew Bible. In 2 Sam 12:13-14, Nathan spoke to David:

> Now the Lord has put away your sin; you shall not die. Nevertheless, because by this deed you have utterly scorned the Lord, the child that is born to you shall die. (NRSV)

In 1 Kgs 21:29, the word of the Lord came to Elijah:

> Have you seen Ahab has humbled himself before me? Because he has humbled himself before me, I will not bring the disaster in his days; but in his son's days I will bring the disaster on his house. (NRSV)

2. Num 14:18

יְהוָה אֶרֶךְ אַפַּיִם וְרַב־חֶסֶד נֹשֵׂא עָוֹן וָפָשַׁע
וְנַקֵּה לֹא יְנַקֶּה פֹּקֵד עֲוֹן אָבוֹת עַל־בָּנִים
עַל־שִׁלֵּשִׁים וְעַל־רִבֵּעִים:

> The LORD is slow to anger, and abounding in steadfast love, forgiving iniquity and transgression, but by no means clearing the guilty, visiting the iniquity of the parents upon the children to the third and the fourth generation. (NRSV)

---

[5] Baruch A. Levine, *Numbers 1-20*, The Anchor Bible (New York: Doubleday, 1993), 381.

This passage is arranged in the context of the Israel's lack of faith caused from the spies' discouraging report about Canaan. It is very likely that this passage derived from Exod 34:6c-7. These two passages show verbal correspondence to each other except for several words that only appear in the Exodus passage.

Exod 34:6c-7

(יְהוָה) ... אֶרֶךְ אַפַּיִם וְרַב־חֶסֶד וֶאֱמֶת:
נֹצֵר חֶסֶד לָאֲלָפִים נֹשֵׂא עָוֹן וָפֶשַׁע וְחַטָּאָה וְנַקֵּה לֹא
יְנַקֶּה פֹּקֵד עֲוֹן אָבוֹת עַל־בָּנִים וְעַל־בְּנֵי בָנִים
עַל־שִׁלֵּשִׁים וְעַל־רִבֵּעִים:

Numbers 14:18

יְהוָה אֶרֶךְ אַפַּיִם וְרַב־חֶסֶד נֹשֵׂא עָוֹן וָפָשַׁע וְנַקֵּה לֹא
יְנַקֶּה פֹּקֵד עֲוֹן אָבוֹת עַל־בָּנִים עַל־שִׁלֵּשִׁים
וְעַל־רִבֵּעִים:

Only those words which I have highlighted in bold in the Exodus passage above are omitted in the Numbers passage, which indicates that the Numbers passage is a short form of the Exodus passage.

3. Exod 20:5c-6 and Deut 5:9c-10

Exod 20:5c-6

כִּי אָנֹכִי יְהוָה אֱלֹהֶיךָ אֵל קַנָּא פֹּקֵד עֲוֹן אָבֹת
עַל־בָּנִים עַל־שִׁלֵּשִׁים וְעַל־רִבֵּעִים לְשֹׂנְאָי:
וְעֹשֶׂה חֶסֶד לַאֲלָפִים לְאֹהֲבַי וּלְשֹׁמְרֵי מִצְוֹתָי:

"Transgenerational Punishment in the Hebrew Bible"

> For I the LORD your God am a jealous God, punishing children for the iniquity of parents, to the third and the fourth generation of those who reject me, ⁶but showing steadfast love to the thousandth generation of those who love me and keep my commandments. (NRSV)

The same passage appears in Deut 5:9c-10. In both cases this passage functions to explain a reason for the second commandment of the Decalogue, the prohibition of making idols and serving them. There are two different points in this retribution formula in comparison with that of Exod 34:6c-7 and Num 14:18. First, the order of cursing and blessing is reversed, and secondly, the phrases לְשֹׂנְאָי ("of those who reject me") and וּלְשֹׁמְרֵי מִצְוֹתָי לְאֹהֲבַי ("of those who love me and keep my commandments") are added as conditional modifiers. For the first point, Jacob Milgrom explains convincingly:

> For when Moses pleads for God's mercy (Exod 34; Num 14), he hides the principle of retribution at the end, but when God states the consequences of defection from His worship in the Decalogue, he states the principle of retribution first.⁶

The addition of modifiers, לְשֹׂנְאָי and וּלְשֹׁמְרֵי מִצְוֹתָי לְאֹהֲבַי, leaves ambiguity for exegesis. Syntactically those modifiers can go with 'parents' or 'children' or both. If the modifiers modify 'parents' the passage would support collectivism, but if they modify 'children,' the passage would be balanced with individualism. If the modifiers are related to both, the connotation of the passage would be standing between the two previous positions, collectivism and collectivism balanced individualism. On the issue of this ambiguity, I prefer the "children" option to the others for two reasons. First, לְשֹׂנְאָי is located right next to רִבֵּעִים עַל־בָּנִים עַל־שִׁלֵּשִׁים וְעַל rather than אָבֹת. If לְשֹׂנְאָי goes with

---

⁶ Jacob Milgrom, *Numbers*, The JPS Torah Commentary (Philadelphia: The Jewish Publication Society, 1990), 395.

'children' לְאֹהֲבַי וּלְשֹׁמְרֵי מִצְוֹתָי, which also located right next to לַאֲלָפִים, modifies the 'children'. Second, when we consider the reason for the adding of modifiers to the older formula of Exod 34:6c-7, the editor would have had an intention of qualification by using the modifier. If we take the other two options, there is no difference between the older formula and the modified formula in terms of its implication. In that case, both formulae signify collective retribution transgenerationally. Thus, when we consider the editor's intention of the addition of modifiers, it is more plausible to relate the modifiers to 'children' rather than to 'parents' or to both 'parents and children.'

When the complimentary modifiers are related to 'children,' the cursing and blessing of the ancestors will be perpetuated, on the condition that the descendants follow the same way of their ancestors. In terms of message, Exod 20:5c-6 and Deut 5:9c-10 lessen the burden of the issue of divine justice. It seems more understandable and fairer to allow for the cursing and blessing of the descendants when they, themselves, deserve that cursing or blessing, rather than receiving it just because of the work of their ancestors.

אֲלָפִים is 'thousandth', as in the 'thousandth generation', rather than 'thousands', because it forms a symmetry of a formula with עַל־בָּנִים עַל־שִׁלֵּשִׁים וְעַל־רִבֵּעִים. In addition, the אֲלָפִים is not for sinners but for those who love God and keep his commandments as in Deut 7:9. The numerical difference between 'thousandth' and 'fourth' indicates God's kindness exceeding his wrath.

4. Deut 24:16

לֹא־יוּמְתוּ אָבוֹת עַל־בָּנִים וּבָנִים לֹא־יוּמְתוּ
עַל־אָבוֹת אִישׁ בְּחֶטְאוֹ יוּמָתוּ׃

> Parents shall not be put to death for their children, nor shall children be put to death for their parents; only for their own crimes may persons be put to death. (NRSV)

At the first glace it seems that Deut 24:16 is contradictory to Deut 5:9c-10 with which we have just dealt. How can these two seemingly contradictory passages exist in the same book? On this question, scholars generally solve the question by answering that Deut 5:9c-10 applies to the divine-human relationship while Deut 24:16 relates to human jurisprudence.[7] In other words, the former is about sin and the latter is concerned with crime. It is an appropriate distinction when we think of the context of each passage. The passages of Exod 34:7, Num 14:8, Exod 20:5c-6 and Deut 5:9c-10, where people's sins of making idols and serving other gods appear, apply to the divine-human relationship. Deut 24:16, however, occurs in the middle of the context of various human regulations in a community. The passage of 2 Kgs 14:6, which quotes Deut 24:16, also relates to jurisprudence of human authority. In 2 Kgs 14:6, Amaziah, son of Joash, executed the officials who assassinated his father, but he did not put the sons of the assassins to death based on the law prescribed in Deut 24:16. For the distinction between 'sin' and 'crime,' the distinction of vocabularies does not help. The word, חטא, used in the context of human jurisprudence in Deut 24:16, is also used in the passage of the divine-human relationship in Exod 34:7.

5. Lev 26:39

---

[7] Richard D. Nelson, *Deuteronomy*, Old Testament Library (Louisville: Westminster John Knox Press, 2002), 292. Jeffrey H. Tigay, *Deuteronomy*, The JPS Torah Commentary (Philadelphia: Jewish Publication Society, 1996), 436. S. R. Driver, *Deuteronomy*, The International Critical Commentary (New York: Charles Scribbner's Sons, 1906), 277-278.

וְהַנִּשְׁאָרִים בָּכֶם יִמַּקּוּ בַּעֲוֺנָם בְּאַרְצֹת אֹיְבֵיכֶם
וְאַף בַּעֲוֺנֹת אֲבֹתָם אִתָּם יִמָּקּוּ׃

And those of you who survive shall languish in the land of your enemies because of their iniquities; also they shall languish because of the iniquities of their ancestors. (NRSV)

This passage is a part of God's warning for Israelites' disobedience to God. As Jeffrey Tigay states, this verse is the middle ground between transgenerational retribution and the individual punishment. [8] If the following generations are disobedient to God, as their ancestors were, they too will suffer because the sins of both themselves and their ancestors.

6. Jer 31:29-30

בַּיָּמִים הָהֵם לֹא־יֹאמְרוּ עוֹד אָבוֹת אָכְלוּ בֹסֶר
וְשִׁנֵּי בָנִים תִּקְהֶינָה׃ כִּי אִם־אִישׁ בַּעֲוֺנוֹ יָמוּת
כָּל־הָאָדָם הָאֹכֵל הַבֹּסֶר תִּקְהֶינָה שִׁנָּיו׃

In those days they shall no longer say: "The parents have eaten sour grapes, and the children's teeth are set on edge." ³⁰But all shall die for their own sins; the teeth of everyone who eats sour grapes shall be set on edge. (NRSV)

This is a part of Jeremiah's prophecy for the future restoration of Judah and Israel. In this prophecy God proclaims that individuals are the ones who are solely responsible for their own deeds in the divine-human relationship as the law of human

---

[8] Tigay, 437.

jurisprudence requires. The phrase, לֹא־יֹאמְרוּ עוֹד indicates the change of the retribution principle. As the new covenant was promised right next to this passage, God promised a new principle on the issue of collective retribution. In the past there was room for transgenerational punishment, particularly when the following generations kept the sinful paths of their ancestors. More accurately, when the following generations, up to the fourth, continued to commit sins, the cursing of their father would be added. However, in the coming days when Judah and Israel are restored, the chain of transgenerational punishment would not exist as the law of human jurisprudence.

7. Lam 5:7

אֲבֹתֵינוּ חָטְאוּ אֵינָם אֲנַחְנוּ עֲוֹנֹתֵיהֶם סָבָלְנוּ׃

> Our ancestors sinned; they are no more, and we bear their iniquities. (NRSV)

There is a tone of indignant revolt toward God for the exilic situation of Israel.[9] The textual trace of וַ added to אֲנַחְנוּ carries a strong disjunctive sense and this sense reinforces the Israelites' indignant revolt.[10] Interestingly, this complaint is balanced with the following confession in Lam 5:16:

> The crown has fallen from our head; woe to us, for we have sinned. (NRSV)

---

[9] Walther Zimmerli, *Ezekiel 1*, Hermeneia (Philadelphia: Fortress Press, 1979), 378.
[10] F. W. Dobbs-Allsopp, *Lamentations*, Interpretation (Louisville, John Knox Press, 2002), 146.

These two balanced statements remind us of Exod 20:5-6 (Deut 5:9-10), where the visiting of the ancestors' iniquity to the disobedient descendants is mentioned. Jer 16:10-12 corresponds well to the background of the two statements:

> And when you tell this people all these words, and they say to you, "Why has the LORD pronounced all this great evil against us? What is our iniquity? What is the sin that we have committed against the LORD our God?" then you shall say to them: It is because your ancestors have forsaken me, says the LORD, and have gone after other gods and have served and worshiped them, and have forsaken me and have not kept my law; and because you have behaved worse than your ancestors, for here you are, every one of you, following your stubborn evil will, refusing to listen to me. (NRSV)

8. Ezek 18:2-4

מַה־לָּכֶם אַתֶּם מֹשְׁלִים אֶת־הַמָּשָׁל הַזֶּה
עַל־אַדְמַת יִשְׂרָאֵל לֵאמֹר אָבוֹת יֹאכְלוּ בֹסֶר
וְשִׁנֵּי הַבָּנִים תִּקְהֶינָה: חַי־אָנִי נְאֻם אֲדֹנָי יְהוִה
אִם־יִהְיֶה לָכֶם עוֹד מְשֹׁל הַמָּשָׁל הַזֶּה בְּיִשְׂרָאֵל:
הֵן כָּל־הַנְּפָשׁוֹת לִי הֵנָּה כְּנֶפֶשׁ הָאָב וּכְנֶפֶשׁ הַבֵּן
לִי־הֵנָּה הַנֶּפֶשׁ הַחֹטֵאת הִיא תָמוּת:

> What do you mean by repeating this proverb concerning the land of Israel, "The parents have eaten sour grapes, and the children's teeth are set on edge"? ³As I live, says the Lord GOD, this proverb shall no more be used by you in Israel. ⁴Know that all lives are mine; the life of the parent as well as the life of the child is mine: it is only the person who sins that shall die. (NRSV)

Individual responsibility against collective retribution reaches its climax in Ezek 18. In Ezek 18:2-4, the proverb, which was also used in Jer 31:29-30, functions to support individual responsibility in the divine-human relationship. A different point of Ezek 18:2-4 compared to Jer 31:29-30 is about the timing of the application of the new principle concerning retribution. While Jeremiah proclaims the new principle in the coming day when Judah and Israel are restored, Ezekiel applies the new principle from his present time.

The use of the proverb in Ezekiel's time implies the widespread view of the Israelites that their exilic situation was caused by the sins of their ancestors. This view is also reflected in the Deuteronomistic history (2 Kgs 21), which attributes the fall of Jerusalem to the sins of Manasseh, rather than solely the deeds of the people who lived at the time of fall of Jerusalem. This fatalistic view discouraged the Israelites and resulted in the complaints of the Israelites: "The way of the Lord is unfair" (Ezek 18:25). In this historical context, Ezekiel proclaimed Yahweh's new principle on the retribution issue. Michael Fishbane's comment is appropriate for the background the new principle:

> In presenting this teaching, the prophet Ezekiel wished to rebut any notion of religious fatalism or self-satisfied piety; more positively, he wished to generate a new spiritual realism in the nation and enliven the religiously passive and self-satisfied with the ever-renewed challenge of righteousness.[11]

For the new principle of retribution in the divine-human relationship (Ezek 18:20, "The person who sins shall die. A child shall not suffer for the iniquity of a parent, nor a parent suffer for the iniquity of a child"), it seems that Ezekiel uses the formula of the retribution of human jurisprudence stated in Deut 24:16 as Moshe Greenberg noted.[12]

---

[11] Michael Fishbane, "Sin and Judgment in the Prophecies of Ezekiel," *Interpretation* 38 (1984), 142.

[12] Moshe Greenberg, *Ezekiel 1-20*, Anchor Bible Commentary (New York: Doubleday, 1983), 333.

Deut 24:16			Ezek 18:20
not fathers for sons	1	3	the one who sins dies
not sons for fathers	2	2	not son for father
each dies for his own sins	3	1	not father for son

As Greenberg noticed, the normal sequence 'fathers-son' appears in Deuteronomy and the reversed order appears in Ezekiel; this suggests that Ezekiel borrowed Deuteronomy.[13] Finally, the two different retribution formulae of the divine-human relationship and human jurisprudence became one and the same formula in Ezekiel.

Conclusion

I arranged the most crucial retribution passages in the Hebrew Bible, according to what is in my view their most likely chronological order, and examined them to find out the most plausible way of understanding the theme of retribution in the Hebrew Bible. As the analysis of passages showed, the relationship and the messages of the eight passages are complex and interrelated. It cannot be simply said that the retribution passages of the Hebrew Bible are contradictory and inconsistent with each other. The following is my suggestion for understanding the theme of retribution based on the text of the Hebrew Bible.

Exod 34:7 and Num 14:18, the shorter form of Exod 34:7, concern God's exceptional 'חֶסֶד' for the thousands (אֲלָפִים) of people who committed sins against God. In the two passages, the way of God's 'loving-kindness' is expressed in delaying the punishment of the sinners to their descendants. Although from the side of the descendants, God's way of exercising His loving-

---

[13] Ibid.

kindness looks unfair, the Hebrew Bible text just states that that is the way of God's loving-kindness. Within the second commandment of the Decalogue (Exod 20:5-6 and Deut 5:9-10), the phrase "of those who reject me" modifies children, such that God's transgenerational punishment would be laid upon the descendants when the descendants disobey God's commandments as their fathers had done.

In Deut 24:6, the emphasis on individual responsibility applies to human jurisprudence. In Lev 26:39, collective retribution and individual responsibility are balanced as Exod 20:5. Lam 5:7 is to be viewed in conjunction with the following verse, 5:16. Those two verses indicate that the exilic Israelites bore their own iniquities, as well as that of their fathers. In Jer 31 and Ezek 18 individual responsibility arrives at the peak of the retribution discussion. Jeremiah proclaims the new principle of individual responsibility in the future when Judah and Israel are restored. This future prophecy was fulfilled in Ezekiel's present time before the restoration, to prohibit the severe fatalism of the Israelites. The new principle's verbal correspondence with Deut 24:16 betrayed that at the time of Ezekiel, the retribution principle in the divine-human relationship had finally become the same as the principle of human jurisprudence. In this new principle any trace of transgenerational punishment (e.g., Exod 20:5) is removed, and becomes congruent with the principle of human jurisprudence that strictly emphasizes individual responsibility.

Yong-Sun Yang

"Economics and Theology of Salvation In Adam Smith and Hegel"[1]

Yong-Sun Yang

Abbreviations used in the paper

WN   *An Inquiry into the Nature and Causes of the Wealth of Nations*
TMS *The Theory of Moral Sentiments*
PR   *Elements of the philosophy of right*

I. Introduction

What has theology to do with economics? Economics is usually regarded as a value-free science dealing with facts, while theology is a value-laden science searching for spiritual truth. Economic man is assumed to be a rational being looking for maximization of self-interest, a religious man is believed to be a self-sacrificing man devoting one's life for the benefit of others. There seems to be a big gap between economics and theology in understanding who we are and what we want. Two anthropologies in economics and theology seem to be so different that it seems to be beyond our ability to communicate on the same horizon.

---

[1] This academic paper was delivered at the 2008 Australian and New Zealand Association of Theological Schools (ANZATS) annual conference in Auckland, New Zealand.

However, salvation is a possible issue shared between economics and theology as we all have a natural desire for happiness in this world and in a life to come. Salvation cannot be an exclusive issue either for economics or for theology in the sense that humans have a desire for salvation not only in body but also in mind and spirit as well. Consequently, salvation is a proper place from which to start for a meaningful conversation between economics and theology. In this paper, salvation is chosen as a commonly shared foundation on which economics and theology stands together so that we may analyse the theological foundations of the economic ideas of Adam Smith and Hegel. It is argued that the divine–human interaction around salvation is explicable both theologically and as rational economic action, and further that combining these two perspectives enriches our understanding of salvation.

II. Self-Interest as a Way of Salvation

Self-interest is like a prism which shows various colours depending on which position we take. It has a broad range of meanings from rationality to a blind selfishness. The various colours of self-interest are sometimes the reason why there are difficulties and misunderstanding in dialogue between economics and theology. Self-interest as the human desire of bettering one's condition for happiness is quite often identified and criticised as selfishness, a blind self-autonomy, and a distorted self-love against others-interest, social welfare. God-love is one of many examples in the Bible showing that self-interest seems to have various dimensions. Prayer is an expression of human desire for salvation. In the Christian Lord's Prayer, there are at least three different levels of the self-conscious desires: daily bread at an economical level, forgiveness at a moral level, and deliverance at a theological level.

Various Approaches to Self-Interest

Wogaman (1986) argues that individualism based on self-interest points out the destructive possibilities of self-centred behaviour such as motivating people through their insecurities and vulnerabilities. In this critique, the point is not in self-interest itself but in the negative side of self-interest, that is, selfishness. Rationality and selfishness are regarded as two different faces of self-interest, and they stand on the same horizon of salvation, moving in a similar direction. This approach has a belief that there is a possibility of harmony between individual interest and social welfare. Self-interest has both merits and demerits in it, so there is a possibility of correcting the faulty side of self-interest such as selfishness for social welfare. This critique is concerned about the tension between individual benefit and social welfare, not denying the positive role of self-interest. The point of this critique is then in the question of whether individualism of self-interest is solipsistic or relational.

MacIntyre (1981) argues that an autonomous human has no future because there is no *telos* in the human autonomy based on self-interest. According to his critique, human self-autonomy rejects any teleological view of man. His critique comes from a philosophical perspective that rational self-interest has neither virtue nor future because it has no essence that defines human true end. He argues that we need the law of God requiring a new kind of respect and awe rather than the self-autonomy based on self-interest as he believes that the true end of man can no longer be completely achieved in this world. According to his philosophical critique against rationality of self-interest, Adam Smith is a deist rather than a Christian as Adam Smith's moral philosophy is based on self-command which enables to control our passions when virtue requires for social welfare. His conclusion is that self-interest is to fail because it has no teleological virtue that leads to future. Similarly, Long (2000) also says that the modern rationality dissolves all goodness and beauty into interest so it lacks virtue to find out God, the ultimate end. In these philosophical critiques, the point is not in the negative side of self-interest but in the blindness of the human rationality based on self-interest. According to these critiques, virtue and autonomous reason are two different faces of self-interest, and they may stand on the same horizon of salvation but move in an opposite direction. If we follow the human self-autonomy of self-interest, according to these critiques, there is no salvation for individuals and society because there is no future and *telos* in rational self-interest. The issue of this philosophical critique is then in the question of whether self-interest has virtue or teleological future in it.

In addition to these economic and moral approaches, there is a theological approach to self-interest. Milbank (1990) argues that MacIntyre's moral virtue is insufficient in refuting secular reason as human autonomy is only a myth which can not be refuted but out-narrated by a better story. Virtue is, according to his theological critique, another conflict as long as it is a matter of overcoming less virtue. The circulation of conflict of virtue cannot be overcome by virtue, so he argues that virtue is not such a scarce resource as assumed in the modern naked competition in capitalism. Therefore, according to him, MacIntyre's argument of virtue is a reward for excellence rather than a free gift. By arguing for a theological dimension of self-interest, he disconnects completely self from interest which is connected in MacIntyre's argument of a rewarding virtue. According to Milbank, virtue is not self-interest of human beings but a gift from God, so there is no possibility of self-interest being a competitive virtue at all. Following this line of argument, he concludes that capitalism based on rational self-interest is a heresy celebrating human autonomy, which is motivated by will for interest, and not by a true, good, and beautiful gift from God because human economic behaviours are not any more aesthetic or liturgical work offered to God but a sacrifice made by my will for wages as a reward. This critique stands on a different horizon from the economical and philosophical approaches mentioned above. Not only that human autonomy based on rational self-interest has no virtue or future, but it is also heretical from his theological point of view. In this critique, virtue and gift are two different faces of self-interest. They stand on two different horizons parallel to each other with no possibility of coming together like heaven and earth. One is the horizon of gift leading to the grace of God, while the other is the horizon of virtue leading to heretical damnation. The issue of this theological critique against self-interest is then the question of whether self-interest is a gift from God.

Adam Smith's Self-Interest

Adam Smith believes that self-interest is a way of salvation for individuals and society. We are self-conscious human beings who have an interest in ourselves. Be it positive or negative, we are always concerned about ourselves. For Adam Smith, the desire of the single minded pursuit of self-interest is a human nature given by God's providence, which is neither a moral failure nor a religious disobedience. Humans are born with natural self-consciousness of bettering one's condition for their own happiness. In his theology of economics, the seemingly economic behaviour is in essence related to a theological faith. It would be inaccurate to describe Adam Smith's self-interest as purely a matter of human autonomy without a theological dimension, for Adam Smith believes that "all the events in this world were conducted by the providence of a wise, powerful, and good God, and we might be assured that whatever happened tended to the prosperity and perfection of the whole" (TMS VII.ii.I.18). Adam Smith's faith that self-interest is inherent in human nature by God's providence cannot be a garment to be dispensed with; rather, it is a pivotal essence in his whole system of thought, including all human behaviours, no matter it be economic, moral or religious. In his theology of economics, human self-interest is a natural instinct given by God's providence, so he believes that self-interest is a way of salvation for individuals and society.

Adam Smith's self-interest is therefore more than Hirschman's 'calm passion' (1977), Myers' 'the soul of modern economic man' (1983) or MacIntyre's secular reason (1981; MacIntyre 1988). Smith's self-interest has its own *telos* in God's providence. He believes that self-interest is not something to be acquired neither from inside nor outside; rather, it is a natural gift endowed by the benevolent Creator, for Adam Smith says that the desire of self-preservation is proposed in the formation of humans for their own sakes without any consideration of its tendency to the beneficent ends which God intends to produce (TMS II.i.5.10). According to his theological foundation of his economic ideas, the human self-conscious desire does not dissolve goodness and beauty into a distorted self-love; rather, self-interest originates from the goodness of God as Nature has directed us by original and immediate instinct. Kleer (2000), Hill (2001; Hill and Lunn 2004), and Alvey (2004) also discusses the role of teleological nature of self-interest in Adam Smith's works.

If Knight (1939) criticises against the lack of reality in Christian love, then Adam Smith may say that the self-interest on which modern economics are believed to stand on is essentially a matter of sympathy coming from self-love (TMS IV.iii.1.4). Wogaman's critique against the weakness of human centeredness of falling into blind selfishness is not neglected in Adam Smith's self-interest that has three levels of moral structure as discussed by Halteman (2003). If self-interest is criticized for its weakness of falling into selfishness, Adam Smith may come forward with a bond and union of friendship of trade and a moral system of sympathy, the impartial spectator, and the still-higher tribunal (TMS IV.iii.c.9; TMS III.2.33-34; TMS III. 3.20-23, 28-29). Solipsistic selfishness may be corrected into relational union through self-interest in the market through which Adam Smith believes that even the smallest parts are fitted to one another and will contribute to compose one immense and connected system (WN II.ii.13-16). If Milbank points out the limitation of human virtue as a way of salvation and suggests a theological interpretation of trade in terms of a gracious free gift rather than the narrow selfishness of contract, then Adam Smith observes the unstableness and ineffectiveness of both human passion and virtue and says about the benevolence of God. He may speak about the inherent instinct of self-interest given by divine providence, which may be for him a higher dimension of inherent human quality than "feeble effort of human reason" and "uncertain determination of our reason" (WN V.i.g.24-25; TMS II.i.5.8-10). A divinely given instinct of self-interest may guide the tension between passion and virtue into harmony. If self-interest is criticised as heretical secular reason from a Christian point of view as MacIntyre talks about the lack of teleology in human autonomous reason from an eschatological perspective of salvation, Adam Smith does not put faith in feeble human reason; he may say that self-interest is a providential gift as embedded in human instinct and that God guides this self-interest by the invisible hand making "ample provision for remedying many of the bad effects of the folly and injustice of man" (WN IV.ix.28).

Hegel's Self-Consciousness

Hegel's approach to self-interest is in essence theological because the biblical concept of original sin is a theological foundation of his economic thoughts. Hegel believes that self-interest as a natural instinct is related to original sin of humans. Nature, in his thoughts, is evil to be overcome by human reason. According to him, humans are born with natural instinct that should be controlled by rational reason. He believes that the natural desire of self-interest is nothing but original sin. Hegel's economic approach to self-interest is essentially theological as it is related to original sin. In Hegel's thoughts, human nature is evil unless it is cultivated by the development of self-consciousness through the ethical life. Nature is bad and reason is good. The human desire of self-interest is a natural instinct, so it is an evil to be overcome in the civil society. For Hegel, the economic desire of self-interest as a natural instinct is related to original sin:

> The Christian doctrine that man is by nature evil is superior to the other according to which he is good. Interpreted philosophically, this doctrine should be understood as follows. As spirit, man is a free being who is in a position not to be determined by natural drives. When he exists in an immediate and uncivilized condition, he is therefore in a situation in which he ought not to be, and from which he must liberate himself. This is the meaning of the doctrine of original sin, without which Christianity would not be the religion of freedom. (Hegel, Wood et al. 1991)

Hegel's self-interest is a human consciousness embedded in human nature as in Adam Smith, who puts self-interest at the centre of motivating power for human relationships in the market. However, in Hegel's theology of economics, the desire of self-interest is an evil to be overcome because it is the natural instinct of humans. In Hegel's theological paradigms, humans are created to be able to choose between good and evil. Hegel's attitude to the role of human self-interest for social welfare is dialectical as he believes that self-interest is a natural desire that should be preserved in the market for individuals to maximise their own interest, yet it should be also overcome as well by an ethical life in the state. The seeming contradiction in Hegel's understanding of the role of self-interest for human happiness is related with his theological preconception that human desire of self-interest is based on human nature which is bad in essence. According to his own theological interpretation of original sin in the biblical story, he presumes that human desire of self-interest is a natural instinct to be overcome by rational self-consciousness. The natural instinct of self-interest in Hegel's economic thoughts is founded on an essentially theological presumption which is open to theological questions.

His solution is that the religious myth of original sin is to be rationally understood only when both the negative and the positive springs from the same root. According to him, it is because we can tell the difference between good and evil that we can be good.

> Religious myth tells us that man is like God in his knowledge of good and evil, and this likeness is indeed present in that the necessity here is not a natural necessity- on the contrary, the decision is in fact the cancellation of this duality of good and evil (PR 139 Addition).

Therefore, according to Hegel, ethical life is to overcome this mere one-sided abstraction of self-certainty by rational self-consciousness of mutual recognition between evil and good. From this ethical approach to the meaning of the original sin, Hegel faces squarely the never-ending question regarding the relationship between fact and value, nature and spirit, faith and knowledge, and evil and good with rational self-consciousness.

For Hegel, falling into the level of a personal feeling is nothing but an abstractive imagination far away from reality. He does not want to explain away the tension between good and evil by saying that truth itself cannot be known. For Hegel, truth is not in individual's heart, emotion and enthusiasm (PR Preface). His bold argument that evil and good is indivisible is the result of his rational explanation of the religious myth of the original sin as he believes that self-consciousness knows how to discover a positive aspect in its own end (PR 140). His strong faith in the rational ability of human self-consciousness comes from his theological interpretation of the original sin that good and evil are indivisible just as God is both the absolutely positive and the absolutely negative at the same time. His theology is different from Adam Smith's. God's goodness never fails in Adam Smith's theology of economics; however, Hegel's God is neither good nor evil. This theological difference leads to a different approach to the economic behaviours motivated by the desire of self-interest. In Hegel's theological foundations of economic thoughts, if an economic behaviour is based on natural self-interest, it has an origin of evil in itself and should be overcome at some stage by rational self-consciousness. The validity of Hegel's interpretation of natural self-interest in relation with the original sin is beyond a purely economic perspective as it is in essence a theological issue regarding who God is. We may however conclude that his economic ideas are closely related with his theology as shown in his theological implication of economic self-interest.

Then the next question to be followed is whether or not Hegel's use of self-interest as natural selfishness is on the right track. Of course, it may be a matter of definition and even a language game; however, it cannot be so simply ignored, because there are theological preconceptions in its usage. As mentioned above, for Hegel, self-interest is not only identified with the natural desire such as emotion, opinions, and ignorance, but is also contrasted with rational reason such as ethics, spirit, and laws of right. These arguments are closely related to his own theological interpretation of the original sin in the biblical story. Only rational humans, according to him, are able to tell the difference between good and evil, which are originally interpenetrated to each other from the beginning of the creation rather than evil is attached later to good from outside by God's passive permission. He argues:

> If we presuppose that, at the creation of the world, God is the absolutely positive, it is impossible to recognize the negative within this positive, no matter which way we turn; for to assume that evil was permitted by God is to assume on his part a passive relationship which is unsatisfactory and meaningless.... But this cannot satisfy thought, which demands a reason and a necessity and seeks to apprehend the negative as itself rooted in the positive.... Since I am confronted with both good and evil, I am able to choose between them; I can choose either of them and accept one or the other into my subjectivity. (PR 139 Addition)

From this theological assumption, he therefore is able to argue that we are free and self-conscious to overcome the duality of evil and good since a human is like God in his knowledge of good and evil.

Our likeness with God in our knowledge of good and evil cannot be in *natural self-interest* which is to be *naturally given* but in *rational self-consciousness* which is to be *consciously achieved*. In brief, his approach to self-interest is founded on his rational interpretation of the original sin.

III. Adam Smith's Salvation and Hegel's Salvation

In this section, the reading of Hegel and Adam Smith from an angle of salvation will show that economical and theological salvation are indivisible as they are intertwined in their thoughts, and that how their theological faiths prop up their economic analysis. The issue of salvation is one of the central notions not only in our daily lives and conversations but also in the works of Adam Smith and Hegel as well, both of whom are deeply concerned about the harmony between individual self-interest and social welfare.

Is Salvation Individual or Communal?

If salvation is to be saved from economic, moral, or theological evil, then a question we may think of is whether it is individual or communal. Hegel argues that salvation is to be achieved in this world rather than in a life to come as the state is the march of God in the world.

> The state in and for itself is the ethical whole, the actualisation of freedom, and it is the absolutely end of reason that freedom should be actual. The state is the spirit which is present in the world and which consciously realises itself therein, whereas, it actualises itself only as the other of itself…. The state consists in the march of God in the world…. (PR 258 addition)

"Economics and Theology of Salvation in Adam Smith and Hegel"

In Hegel, salvation cannot be separate from economic justice in the world since God is immanent in the world. Economic justice for salvation is the most essential issue for Hegel to achieve not only the social welfare but also the personal happiness itself as well. Therefore, if national economic growth is not justified by personal happiness, it has no meaning at all because God is to be realised not by economic growth but by personal self-consciousness. The rational self-consciousness cannot be realised unless there is economic justice in the world. That is the reason the ethical state is required to be the essential moment of the ethical life in the world where God is immanent. Salvation is the universal good *to be achieved in the world* by development of individual self-consciousness in the ethical state which is the march of God who is to be realised through self-autonomy of individuals. In Hegel, salvation is in essence social freedom; freedom cannot be achieved without the development of self-consciousness transcending the laws of nature.

However, the story is the complete opposite to the case of Adam Smith who believes that the ultimate salvation is not in this world but in a life to come:

> Our happiness in this life is thus, upon many occasions, dependent upon the humble hope and expectation of a life to come: a hope and expectation deeply rooted in human nature; which can alone support its lofty ideas of its own dignity; can alone illumine the dreary prospect of its continually approaching mortality, and maintain its cheerfulness under all the heaviest calamities to which, from the disorders of this life, it may sometimes be exposed. There is a world to come, where exact justice will be done to every man.... (TMS III.2.33)

Believing in a transcendent God, he is able to be freed from the shackle of our duty to achieve the universal good in the world, for our salvation is not necessarily contingent on the economic and ethical life. This theological difference between them is the pivotal point to understand the difference of the economic and moral ideas between Hegel and Adam Smith. In Adam Smith's God, God is transcendent; however, God never fails in his goodness, so we are never God-forsaken in this world. The proof of God being with us in his never-failing goodness is an inherent desire of self-interest by the wisdom of Nature in Adam Smith's thoughts. By this, Adam Smith connects human self-interest with God's transcendence through the nature of wisdom. Adam Smith accepts human weakness as natural; however, he believes that human weakness is the grace of God who never fails to take care of the world. Therefore, we may conclude that in Adam Smith a true salvation is not something to be achieved in the world by the development of self-consciousness but *to be given in a life to come individually*. Of course, Adam Smith argues that our effort for happiness in this world is important not only for ourselves but also for others for he believes that the great Author our nature will render to everyone to the works he performed in this world.

> When we thus despair of finding any force upon earth which can check the triumph of injustice, we naturally appeal to heaven, and hope, that the great Author of our nature will himself execute hereafter, what all the principles which he has given us for the direction of our conduct, prompt us to attempt even here.... and will, in a life to come, render to every one according to the works which he has performed in this world. (TMS III 5.10)

However, the point of Adam Smith's argument is that salvation is open to everyone regardless of whether he is poor or rich, or whether the civil society has in itself ethical defects or not. Adam Smith would say that what is not possible with man is possible with God for salvation is in essence in a life to come; however, Hegel would say that what is not possible in man is not possible with God either, since salvation is essentially in this world. In Adam Smith, we are individually free in our desire of searching for self-interest; however, the true happiness is only in a life to come.

Different theology leads to different economics. In Hegel, we cannot be free unless we are social as our consciousness is something to be realised in relationship with others, for salvation is in essence communally realised in the world; however, in Adam Smith, we cannot be social unless we are free as self-interest is something to be given without relationship with others, for salvation is in essence individually received.

Is Salvation God's Grace or Human Achievement?

Hegel's self-consciousness is something *to be realized* by human freedom and will, while Adam Smith's self-interest is something *to be given* in human nature and instinct. This delicate difference between two important thinkers in approaching to the essential motive of human economic behaviours comes from their own anthropology and theology.

Hegel's self-consciousness is as much colourful as Adam Smith's self-interest. Self-consciousness is desire (Hegel, Findlay et al. 1977). Hegel's self-consciousness as desire, however, is not something to be given naturally as in Adam Smith's approach to self-interest which is an inherent instinct given by the Wisdom of God, but something to be realised rationally by reciprocity of interpersonal relationship through mutual recognition

Adam Smith clearly criticises such human consciousness as blinded selfishness in many places of his works. Self-interest for Adam Smith is neither morally degraded selfishness nor ethically neutral rationality; rather, it is an imbedded instinct in man by God's providence. We may assume that one of the reasons why Hegel uses such a negative definition of an economic man in spite of his knowledge of Adam Smith's ideas is because of the necessity of differentiating his ethical life from morality.

For Hegel, self-consciousness is not something to be given to man naturally as laws of nature but to be realised by man as laws of right. This is his vantage point from which he develops his economic and ethical arguments. By using self-consciousness,

Hegel fills the gap between emotional feeling and rational reason and connects the particularity of the family based on the feeling of love and the universality of the state based on the rationality of reason through the mediation of the civil society which is composed with self-conscious individuals whose ends are private, particular, and contingent (PR 185). Hegel's self-consciousness is to be realised, while Adam Smith's self interest is to be given.

Is There Afterlife or No Afterlife?

Hegel is a teleological thinker who has faith in a providential ends in history culminating towards the apex in the state with the cunning of reason as a part of God's self-realising process through the development of rational self-consciousness until God and man achieve self-realisation in the world; therefore, it is rational for him to have faith in the ethical life in the world, not an afterlife above the world. However, Adam Smith is also a teleological thinker who has faith in a divine providence presiding over the world with the unfailing goodness of the invisible hand through natural self-interest of individuals to be given by the wisdom of Nature until we stand before God; therefore, it is natural for him to have faith in the afterlife not the ethical life. It is faith because we cannot prove or disprove until it comes true.

For Hegel, the world is the place where there happens God's self-actualisation through individuals' self-consciousness. The end of the world is the actualisation of God's self-consciousness in men's self-consciousness and the realisation of men's self-consciousness in God's self-consciousness. His eschatology is circular in the sense that God actualises himself through men's self-consciousness, and men realise themselves through God's self-consciousness. For him, God and men are one and the same in the realisation of self-consciousness in his eschatology. This transient world is eternal (PR preface p. 20). For Adam Smith, the world is the place where we stay temporarily with the hope that there is a world to come with true happiness.

Smith's Kingdom of God and Hegel's Kingdom of God

The Kingdom of God is an interesting issue in relation with salvation although the word Kingdom of God is never used in Adam Smith' main works, nor is it used in Hegel's *Philosophy of Right* except in one case when he compares the church and the state, arguing that emotional religion itself should not hold the reins of governments which belongs to the rational state (PR 270 addition). Hegel uses the language of the Kingdom of God in a negative context, and we may understand Hegel's position when we take into account that the state is the divine providence of God in the world for Hegel. In Hegel, there is no kingdom of God without the state which is the divine will as the present spirit (PR 270). The point we can think of is the range of the kingdom of God, in which God rules the world.

In Hegel, there is no idea of a life to come as discussed above, nor is there any room for nature for the end of history through the perfection of man in the state. For him, the supreme manifestation of realisation of God is in the state which is real and rational; therefore, the kingdom of God based religious feeling or emotion is required to give way to the rational state (PR 270). In addition, in Hegel's Kingdom of God, there is no room for people who are regarded as natural or irrational, for example, the children, women and other some ethnic groups (PR 139). Inevitably, we may conclude that Hegel's kingdom of God might be concrete in the state but very narrow in its range.

Compared to Hegel's Kingdom of God, Adam Smith's Kingdom of God seems to be broader than Hegel's Kingdom of God despite the fact that he never uses the language in his main works. If we understand the meaning of the Kingdom of God roughly as the world that God rules over, Adam Smith has two kinds of Kingdom of God compared to Hegel: in this world and in a life to come. In this world, the essence of the kingdom of God is God's grace. Adam Smith describes that our world is filled with the goodness of God, for every part of nature equally demonstrates the providential care of its Author even in the weakness and folly of man (TMS II.iii.3.2). In Adam Smith's Kingdom of God, no one is forlorn out of the Kingdom of God which God rules over with unfailing goodness. In Adam Smith, the desire of self-interest is a gift from the wisdom of Nature as the example of God's caring over the world, rather than human sin to be overcome by reason as in Hegel, so we able to know that we live in the kingdom of God as we all have self-interest. However, in Adam Smith, self-interest is an efficient cause rather than the final cause in the world as there is a life to come (WN V.i.g.1; TMS III.5.12). In the life to come, the essence of the kingdom of God is justice. The true justice and happiness is to be achieved as we will be rewarded in the life to come according to what we have done in this life. Hegel's kingdom of God seems to be something to be achieved in the world by the development of our self-conscious rationality. Hegel's main concern is to explain how to achieve the kingdom of God in this world, so he has no choice but to have faith in the power of human reason to be realised with God's immanence. In Adam Smith, the Kingdom of God is something to be given to the world by the wisdom of Nature in our hope for a life to come where true happiness is to be achieved; therefore, he is at ease with human nature in this kingdom of God until we reach the life to come.

Smith's Love and Hegel's Love

Love is one of the central messages in the Bible. "God is love. Whoever lives in love lives in God, and God in him" (1Jn 4:16). Love is the essence of the Christian faith, and in a sense a way of salvation in so much as salvation is to be with God. However, there are still many questions to be asked frequently in our daily lives. What is love? How do we love? Is the essence of love self-sacrifice or self-awareness? Is the way of love self-interest or self-negation? There is a difference between Adam Smith and Hegel in their understanding of love because the theological foundations of their economic thoughts are different to each other. The essence of Hegel's approach to love is a rational self-realisation, while a natural self-interest is at the centre of Adam Smith's understanding of love. The important but abstract idea of love is clarified in the theological foundations of their economic thoughts. If God is love, it is natural that a different understanding of God leads to different meaning of love. A true love is not emotional but rational for Hegel, while for Adam Smith, a true love is not rational but natural in its essence.

From the perspective of Adam Smith, we cannot love each other unless we love ourselves as love is the human desire which is motivated by self-interest inherent in human nature by the wisdom of Nature. However, Hegel would say that we cannot love each other unless we love others as our desire is to be realised in a higher ethical stage in the community only through self-negation, which is overcoming and preserving self-interest. If Adam Smith says that love is closely related to self-interest, then Hegel would say that love is not possible without self-negation. Hegel's love is something to be achieved by the rational self-consciousness. I love you because I cannot be satisfied without you. There is no guarantee that I will be satisfied and free when I love someone who loves me because my love is dependent on others who may or may not love me. It does not matter whether I am free and content in self-interest.

Adam Smith's Evil and Hegel's Evil

Adam Smith's evil is related to neither the natural desire for self-interest nor economic scarcity, but to self-negligence. His theology of economics stands on the belief that the world is created by the goodness of God. He says that the vices and follies of mankind are a necessary part of God's providence (TMS I.ii.3.4). Hegel's evil, however, is related to original sin which, he argues, is related to human nature as his theology of economics stands on the preconception that this world is in constant movement for perfection, overcoming human natural instinct by rational self-consciousness.

According to Hegel's theology of economic life, the scarcity of economic resources is evil to society as it is the reason of ethical retardation of the poor. The deficiency in the private and public sectors is inevitable because the people are alienated by the systematic failure of the market which creates wealth and poverty at the same time. So it is necessary to let the market create economic wealth freely but with a clear vision of economic justice to be achieved only by the supplementary intervention of the state. Adam Smith, however, would say that poverty is not such an evil to be overcome by the ethical state intervention. The state intervention may open the door to the systematic evil at the sacrifice of individual self-interest which is not only human weakness but also God's grace as well. The intervention of the state is not the desirable end of human history but the loss of the dynamics of human desire. Then the question is whether economic scarcity is evil. From Hegel's perspective, scarcity itself is not evil but becomes evil when the poor are conscious of the feeling of relative loss in their civil rights. According to Adam Smith's idea, scarcity or poverty is not evil for it works for the creation of wealth and stabilisation of society by self-interest. Although Hegel's and Adam Smith's economic ideas regarding evil and sin are heavily influenced by their own theological preconception, we may conclude that scarcity is not evil in their thoughts.

Hegel's analysis of the human weakness is different from Adam Smith's one. For Hegel, human weakness is to be overcome by ethical life, while Smith believes that human weakness is the essence of human being which cannot be negated in this world. The gap between what it is and what it should be is minimised in Adam Smith's idea by accepting human weakness as the goodness of God's providence, while in Hegel, it is to be transcended by God's self-actualisation through human self-consciousness in the world. Humans are weak in the sense that they pursue their own limited self-interest. Self-interest is natural in the sense that the desire is given as nature imbedded in human instinct by the wisdom of Nature. Self-interest is not only the proof of human weakness but also of God's goodness as the Creator. Justice and grace are two faces of the same goodness of God in Adam Smith's thought. Consequently, evil or sin is a matter of human weakness rather than scarcity of resources.

Smith's Invisible Hand and Hegel's Cunning of Reason

In Adam Smith's theology of economics, God is transcendent over the world but works over the world through the invisible hand, while in Hegel's theology of economics, God is immanent in the world and works thorough the cunning of reason. The cunning of reason is often compared with the invisible hand of Adam Smith. Smith's invisible hand is regarded as a problematic or unnecessary expression by many of the mainstream economists who believe that the economic theory of Adam Smith is able to be understood without such a troublesome concept related to God. John B. Davis (1989) argues that there are similarities in the invisible hand of Adam Smith and the cunning of reason of Hegel as they are used as conceptual tools to explain that the action of self interest in the economic world creates something grater than their sum, something desired yet unintended. He also points out that both Adam Smith and Hegel depend on the divine providence through the invisible hand and the cunning of reason respectively because there is no other way available for uniting self-interest and social welfare, especially in case of dealing with a combination between a value-free part and a value-laden whole. In this vein, Davis argues that the invisible hand and the cunning of reason have instability and discourage rational investigation by evading the human responsibility and depending on the divine providence for reconciling the possible confliction between private interest and general welfare.

In contrast to Davis' approach of emphasizing the similarities, Ullmann-Margalit (1997) concentrates on the dissimilarities between the invisible hand and the cunning of reason. She argues that these two ideas serve profoundly different faith despite superficial similarity. On the surface, both ideas have the same focus on the fact that self-interest leads to general welfare by an ultimate design without any individual intention. However, she argues that there is an important difference between the invisible hand and the cunning of reason. Hegel's cunning of reason is applied to the actions of the historical heroes in the spiritual history, and explains how history uses the results of the actions of a few heroic humans to unfold the execution of God's providence, while Adam Smith's invisible hand is related to the social order, and explains how social welfare comes about as the result of the actions of numerous ordinary humans without any purpose whatever.

There are some interesting points in those different approaches to the relationship between the invisible hand and the cunning of reason. Although their conclusions are different in many ways, it is agreed that the cunning of reason and the invisible hand are the conceptual tools with which to find out a solution for the tension between individual passion and social welfare whether it is related to human history in general or social order in particular, or whether it is about a few heroes or many ordinary humans. The difference may be due to their different theologies of economics. The theological foundations of political economic thoughts are at the centre of this issue. Cunning of reason is God's divine providence in the world in Hegel's theology of economics, while the invisible hand is God's divine providence over the world in Adam Smith's theological world. Both Adam Smith's invisible hand and Hegel's cunning of reason are at the centre of their theological foundations of economic thoughts, rather than unnecessary or contradictory irony.

IV. Conclusion

There is a close relationship between economics and theology. The divine–human interaction around salvation is explicable both theologically and as rational economic action, and further that combining these two perspectives enriches our understanding of salvation. Different theology leads to different economics as economic ideas have theological foundations. The argument is developed in relation to two major philosophers Adam Smith and Hegel. Smith's self-interest is a natural instinct embedded in human nature, while Hegel's self-consciousness is a rational ability to be realised. In Adam Smith's theology, self-conscious nature is good as it is given by God whose goodness never fails, so natural self-interest is a way of salvation for Adam Smith. Hegel, however, believes that nature is an evil to be overcome by human reason as it is related to original sin, so the rational self-consciousness overcoming the natural instinct is a way of salvation for Hegel. Consequently, Adam Smith' salvation is something to be given in a world to come, while Hegel's salvation is something to be achieved in this world. This bifurcation comes from three main differences in their theological foundations. Firstly, Adam Smith's God is all-powerful, all-knowing, always good, and transcendent over the world, while Hegel's God is neither good nor bad, neither all-powerful nor all knowing, but immanent in the world. Secondly, the biblical concept of original sin has no place in Adam Smith's understanding of human beings, while it has the central role for Hegel. Thirdly, for Adam Smith, this world is transitory but full of God's providential goodness expressed in the invisible hand, while Hegel's world is real and eternal but in the process of self-realisation with God's providence working through the cunning of reason.

Bibliography

Alvey, J. E. (2004). "The Hidden Theology of Adam Smith: A Belated Reply to Hill." *European Journal for the History of Economic Thought* **11**(4): 623-628.

Davis, J. B. (1989). "Smith's Invisible Hand and Hegel's Cunning of Reason." *International Journal of Social Economics* **16**(6): 50-66.

Halteman, J. (2003). "Is Adam Smith's Moral Philosophy an Adequate Foundation for a Market Economy?" *Markets and Morality* **6**(2): 453-478.

Hegel, G. W. F. (1956). *The Philosophy of History*. New York, Dover.

Hegel, G. W. F., J. N. Findlay, et al. (1977). *Phenomenology of Spirit*. Oxford, Clarendon Press.

Hegel, G. W. F. and T. M. Knox (1948). *Early Theological Writings*. Chicago, Ill., University of Chicago Press.

Hegel, G. W. F. and A. V. Miller (1989). *Hegel's Science of Logic*. Atlantic Highlands, NJ, Humanities Press International.

Hegel, G. W. F., A. V. Miller, et al. (1977). *Phenomenology of Spirit*. Oxford, Oxford University Press.

Hegel, G. W. F., A. W. Wood, et al. (1991). *Elements of the Philosophy of Right*. New York, Cambridge University Press.

Hill, L. (2001). "The Hidden Theology of Adam Smith." *European Journal for the History of Economic Thought* **8**(1): 1-29.

Hill, P. J. and J. Lunn (2004). "Why are Theologians Opposed to Markets. Is Scripture?"

Kleer, R. A. (2000). "The Role of Teleology in Adam Smith's Wealth of Nations." *History of Economics Review* **31**: 14-29.

Long, D. S. (2000). *Divine Economy: Theology and the Market*. London, Routledge.

MacIntyre, A. (1981). *After Virtue - A Study in Moral Theory*. London, Duckworth.

MacIntyre, A. (1988). *Whose Justice? Which Rationality?* Duckworth.

Milbank, J. (1990). *Theology and Social Theory: Beyond Secular Reason*. Oxford, Basil Blackwell.

Smith, A. (1759). *The Theory of Moral Sentiments*. Oxford, Oxford University Press 1975.

Smith, A. (1776). *An Inquiry into the Nature and Causes of the Wealth of Nations*. Oxford, Oxford University Press 1976.

Smith, A. (1795). *Essays on Philosophical Subjects*. Oxford, Oxford University Press.

Ullmann-Margalit (1997). "The Invisible Hand and the Cunning of Reason." *Social Research* **64**(Summer): 182-198.

Wogaman, J. P. (1986). *Economics and Ethics: A Christian Enquiry*. London, SCM.

Young Mog Song

"Exodus Theme in the Book of Revelation 12-13"[1]

Young Mog Song

Introduction

The fact that the Exodus is one of the central patterns for the saving acts of God in both the OT and NT is widely agreed. For the Israel in the OT, the Exodus motif was the paradigm of redemptive historical renewal. For this reason, the Exodus provided the typological expression for all future hope of salvation and served as a theological paradigm to the OT and the NT authors. In this paper, the Exodus theme in the Book of Revelation 12-13 is probed in the following steps: (1) Christ's crucifixion and resurrection as the archetypal Exodus, (2) the chronological fulfillment of Exodus theme in the Bible, and (3) Exodus theme in Revelation 12-13. To investigate the Exodus theme in Revelation 12-13, the intertextual interpretation based on the redemptive historical interpretation will be used.

1. Christ's Crucifixion and Resurrection as the Archetypal Exodus

In this section, the focus will be on the Gospel according to Luke, since Luke clearly introduces the Exodus of Jesus (Lk. 9:31). Broyles (1992:561-562) interprets correctly Luke's peculiarities of the transfiguration, suffering and resurrection of Jesus in respect to the Exodus theme. These peculiarities can be summarized as

---

[1] This academic paper was delivered at the 2008 International Society of Biblical Literature conference in Auckland, New Zealand.

follows: only Luke records that Moses spoke with Jesus of his impending Exodus from Jerusalem. The Passover lamb whose bones are not to be broken (Ex. 12:46) and the blood of the covenant (Ex. 24:8; cf. Lk. 22:20) foreshadow Jesus' sacrificial death, although no explicit reference to the person Moses is made.

In the central section of Luke (9:1-50) Jesus recapitulates and fulfills the Exodus as the prophet like Moses of Deuteronomy (cf. Garrett, 1992:12). This textual context of Luke 9:1-50 shows that the Exodus of Jesus is the watershed and center of his whole work. The fact that just before the journey to Jerusalem Jesus announced his Exodus (Lk. 9:51) has a parallel in the fact that the Exodus just preceded the journey to the Promised Land of Canaan. Jerusalem as the New Canaan is the promised place of the Holy Spirit as the eschatological gift (Lk. 24:49) and the central place of God's redemption for Israel and the Gentiles (Acts 1:8). Through the above typology of Moses and the Exodus theme, it is clear that Luke intends to reveal the suffering, resurrection and glorification of Christ not only as the second Moses but as the one greater than Moses (cf. Garrett, 1990:659). The points of contact between Moses and Jesus noted in Luke are points of continuity in terms of redemption.[2]

2. The Chronological Fulfillment of the Exodus Theme

The collective memory of the Exodus from Egypt shaped accounts of God's past acts of redemption, and provided the

---

[2] When searching for the Exodus theme in the Four Gospels, it is useful to compare Moses, who as the representative of Israel directly received the OT law on Mt. Sinai, with Jesus Christ, who as the Lawgiver proclaimed the law of the eschatological kingdom of God. Christ as the inaugurator of the New Covenant conveys the true meaning of the OT (in the Johannine term ἀλήθεια meaning *truth*, cf. Lk. 24:44). The Exodus theme in Gospels is an important theological paradigm in which the typology of Moses and Jesus comes to the fore, as it sheds light on the redemptive death and resurrection of Christ.

typological expression for all future hope (cf. Garrett, 1990:656). The OT and the NT prophecies and covenants are fulfilled not so much linearly as spirally (cf. Goldsworthy, 1991:76, 92). In other words, that is a progressive-duplicate fulfillment. At this stage, the fulfillment of the Exodus theme will be shown in the chronological order referring to several important redemptive historical events. The fulfillment of the Exodus theme takes place several times both in the pre-Exodus and in the post-Exodus period.

2.1. The Time of the Pre-Exodus

In the time of the Patriarchs, the Exodus theme appeared in the shape of a shadow. Abraham's return from Egypt with spoils was a foretaste of Israel's Exodus by Moses. The Exodus of Joseph's bones into Canaan could be understood in the same context.

The covenant of Abraham and of the Patriarchs was the main motivation for the Exodus (Ex. 2:24-25, cf. Lk. 1:55). Several similarities between the story of Jacob and the Exodus come to light: (1) Jacob's departure from Laban in several texts is understood in terms of the release of a slave like the Israelites. (2) Two verbs (גרשׁ and שָׁלַח) are common and the characteristic terms of the Exodus (Ex. 6:1; cf. Lk. 1:51). (3) Jacob and the Israelites returned to his fatherland Canaan with a wealth of possessions (Ex. 12:36). (4) The division and separation themes appear (Ge. 30:40). (5) The military term is evident (Ge. 32:2; Ex. 12:41; Lk. 1:51-52). (6) The change of identity takes place (Ge. 32:28; Lk. 1:48). Finally, (7) the service to God is emphasized (Ge. 35:14-15; Ex. 8:1; cf. Daube, 1979:63-64).

2.2. The Time of the Exodus by Moses

The Exodus by Moses as an antitype is a fulfillment of the events of the time of the pre-Exodus. The Exodus itself, of course, functions as a pattern or a paradigm for the later salvific acts by God. Thus there remains its consummation, as well as its fulfillment in the person and works of the New Moses, Christ. The fact that the Exodus from Egypt shows a holistic salvation including physical and spiritual aspects foreshadows the holistic redemption by Jesus. The Exodus by Moses is the true beginning of the eschatological Exodus theme.

2.3. The Time of the Judges

The return of the Ark from the Philistines in the time of Judge Samuel (1 Sa. 6:6-21) is redolent of the Exodus theme in that the event recalls the Exodus. There are several parallels between the return of the Ark from the Philistines and the Exodus: (1) God punished the gods of Egypt and of Philistine (Ex. 12:12; 1 Sa. 5:3-4). In other words, the Ark is a terrible guest to the god Dagon. (2) God punished the Philistines by tumors (Ex. 9:10; 1 Sa. 5:6). (3) The notion of service to God appears (1 Sa. 7:3). (4) Similar words, for instance, כחד (to smite, Ex. 9:15; 1 Sa. 5:12) and מַגֵּפָה (plague, Ex. 9:14; 1 Sa. 6:4), appear (Fretheim, 1991:387). And (5) Moses and Samuel as the leaders of Israel are similar (1 Sa. 7:6-9, 15; cf. Daube, 1979:73-74). By recalling the Exodus by Moses, the return of the Ark in the time of the Judges is related with its return in the time of David. In addition, the return of Ruth's family from Moab can be understood in the Exodus.

2.4. The Time of King David

The Exodus and the Davidic covenant are connected to each other: (1) God performed great wonders to rescue his people (2 Sa. 7:23-24). (2) God drove out nations (e.g. Egypt) and their gods before his people. Indeed, the Davidic covenant not only looks back into the Exodus but also foreshadows the eternal Messianic kingdom.

2.5. The Time of the Pre-Babylon Exile and the (Post-) Babylon Exile

2.5.1. The Time of the Pre-Babylon Exile

As Collins (1995:156) holds, apart from Amos (Am. 2:10; 9:7), Micah recites all that God as the Lord of the world has done for Israel during the Exodus and then switches to the persona of the worshipper. During the time of the pre-Babylon Exile, some prophets proclaimed both the moral life and the true worship as the lifestyle of the people of God by recalling the Exodus. Indeed, the Exodus carries moral obligations as a natural lifestyle to the people of God. Here, too, the Exodus functions as a paradigm for the prophets who carried out their office in the time of the pre-Exile. Even in the time of the pre-Exile, the Exodus theme had the notion of universalism. Moreover, the Exodus theme gave birth to the norms for the Israelites who lived as the people of God in the pre-Exile period.

2.5.2. The Time of the (Post-) Babylon Exile

In Isaiah the hope of deliverance from the Exile is shown not only by looking back to the Exodus but also by anticipating the Messianic salvation (Isa. 42:1). One of the important motivations for the liberation from the Exile was the Abrahamic covenant (Isa. 41:8; cf. Collins, 1995:157). For Hosea and Ezekiel, the reminiscences to the Exodus provide the central themes. God will renew his covenant by leading his people again through the wilderness (Hos. 2:14-20). The Exodus furnishes the evidence of God's love for Israel (Hos. 11:1; Ezk. 20). In the post-Exile time, the prophets considered Israel's breach of God's norms, which in a sense came from the Exodus, as the reason for the Babylon Exile.[3]

---

[3] Here the Book of Esther should be kept in mind, because Esther is filled with Exodus motif. Though every detail of the Exodus Pattern is not present in every instance of it, and there are twists in the way the pattern is presented; yet the

2.5.3. The Time of Jesus Christ

Dillard and Longman III (1994:66) elucidate correctly that "many parallels are drawn between the Exodus and Christ's earthly ministry specifically during his Passion. Jesus went to the cross

---

pattern is always obvious and clear. The following is the sequence, as applied to Esther (see Jordan, 1996:1-4):
(1) Some threat, some aspect of sin or of the curse, drives God's people from their home. The sins of Israel drove the Jews into exile in Babylon, which became Persia. (2) During the sojourn in captivity, Eve (i.e. the exiled Jews) is assaulted by the Serpent, who wishes to use her to raise up his own wicked seed. While nothing is said about Ahasuerus' desiring children from Esther, he does take her into his harem because she is beautiful, the same reason Pharaoh took Sarai from Abram in Genesis 12 (one of the earliest Exoduses). In the Esther events, though, there is a twist: the 'attack' on Eve is not really an attack at all, but is something Mordecai and Esther cooperate with. (3) The righteous use 'holy deception' to trick the serpent and protect Eve. Esther tricks Haman into thinking he is going to be honored, and in a way tricks Ahasuerus into a situation where he is confronted with Haman's perfidy. (4) Very often, God's people are enslaved during the sojourn outside the land. In a strict sense, that is not the case in this instance. (5) God brings blessings upon His people during the captivity, but plagues the tyrant, either progressively or as part of the deliverance. Haman notes that the Jews have the blessing of keeping their own laws in the empire of Persia. The destruction of Haman is the plagues on the tyrant. (6) God miraculously intervenes, often with visions to the pagan lord, in order to save His people. The dream given to the pagan lord during the night is, in this case, Ahasuerus' sleepless night during which he is read the chronicles of his reign, and determines to bless Mordecai. (7) Very often the serpent tries to shift blame and accuses the righteous man of being the cause of the difficulty. In Esther 3 Haman insinuates to Ahasuerus that the Jews are troubling his empire. (8) God humiliates the false gods of the enemy. Haman clearly has his own gods; in fact, when he boasts of his glory and praises his own accomplishments, Haman seems to be his own god (Est. 5:11). (9) God's people depart with spoils. Since God wanted the Jews to be 'spread out as the four winds' within the empire, no geographical departure was needed. (10) On the way, God's people are attacked (Ex. 17; 1 Sa. 15). Cyrus has let the people return, which is the initial Exodus. Now the Jews are attacked by Haman the Agagite. (11) Finally, God's people are installed in the Holy Land. Such installment means building God's house out of some of the spoils. The Jews did not personally take the spoils, but set them aside for God.

during the time of Passover. Christ fulfilled the Exodus during his earthly ministry." In fact, Jesus has re-created the New Israel through restoration in his person and works. In a certain sense, the OT Exodus and the later salvations were confined to the restoration. This is proved by the fact that the verb שוב does not mean 'to re-create' but 'to return' or 'to restore' (Job 33:25; Hos. 6:1). Jesus is the leader or the redeemer of a new and final Exodus through which God initiated his trans-historical plan, i.e. the new Messianic era. The coming, person, and works of the Messiah decisively fulfill all the previous Exodus themes and show their consummation implicitly (cf. Kim, 1997:636).

2.5.4. The Time of the Apostles and the Early Church

In the time of the Apostles and the Early Church, the Exodus theme can be understood through the suffering, resurrection, and glorification of Christ. The archetypal Exodus of Christ makes sure the Exodus of the Early Church. The fact is shown by Garrett (1990:670-680), who compares the rescue of Peter (Acts 12:1-24) with both the resurrection of Jesus (Lk. 9:31) and the Exodus. According to her several similarities are: (1) Peter's imprisonment and rescue take place at Passover (Ex. 12; Acts 12:3-4, cf. Lk. 22:1-2). (2) ἀνάστα ἐν τάχει (Acts 12:7) has a close relation with ἀνίστημι which is used to designate God's action of raising Jesus from the dead. (3) The sequence of events after Peter's escape recalls the events immediately following Jesus' resurrection (Acts 12:13-14; cf. Lk. 24:11). (4) The angel's command to Peter to 'dress yourself and put on your sandals' (Acts 12:8) recalls God's instructions to the Israelites in Exodus 12:11. And (5) Acts 12:11 'rescued me from the hand of Herod' runs parallel with the deliverance from the hand of Egyptians (Ex. 3:8). The above similarities demonstrate that the deliverance of Peter enacts the meaning of Jesus' resurrection (i.e. the archetypal Exodus).

2.5.5. Summary

The fulfillment of the Exodus theme takes place in the form of a spiral (and duplicated) according to the development of the redemptive-revelation history. The centre of the fulfillment of the Exodus theme, Jesus Christ, is evident. God has properly applied and has repeatedly fulfilled the Exodus theme into every period with one great watershed, namely the cross and resurrection of Christ as the decisive fulfillment of the theme. Therefore, each fulfillment in every period naturally connected with Christ whether explicitly or implicitly or partially.

3. Exodus Theme in Revelation 12-13

3.1. Exodus theme in the Book of Revelation[4]

In the Book of Revelation the soteriological message is anchored in Jesus Christ's eschatological-salvific works and it is aligned to the blessings which that saving work affords to the universal Church and to the whole creation (Du Rand, 1993:310). According to Jenkins (1972:68, 71) John makes allusions to the Book of Exodus 27 times, particularly the event of the Exodus. John draws images from the past redemptive works of God (e.g. the Exodus) and presents them again as the vehicle of the present moment to encourage his militant community to endure the persecution.

Many parallels between Exodus 15 and Revelation 15 are important: (1) the theme of victory in Exodus 15 becomes the basis

---

[4] In their recent commentary on the NT use of the OT, Beale and McDonough (2007:1082) hold that in Revelation roughly more than half of the OT references are from Psalms, Isaiah, Ezekiel, and Daniel. They also agree that the accounts of the plagues in Exodus are the source of some of the most startling imagery in Revelation. And the theme of the liberation from oppressive rulers is the predominant motif in Exodus and Revelation.

for praise in Revelation 15:3-4 (Mounce, 1983:287). (2) Several terms, e.g. 'glory', 'victory', and 'tabernacle', are common (cf. Ex. 15:11; Rev. 15:4). (3) The entire scene of Revelation 15:2 revives the Israelites standing on the shore of the Red Sea. (4) The seven plagues (Rev. 11:6; 15:8) recall the ten plagues on Egypt. And (5) the universal recognition of Jehovah as the one true God is a common theme of their praises (Ex. 15:14; Rev. 15:4; Mounce, 1983:288).

All the redeemed on earth shall stand at the sea of glass to join the victorious crowd in singing their Song of Moses and of the Lamb. This is supported by the fact that the song which they sing is that of Moses *and* of the Lamb, combining therefore the Old and the NT into one. Moreover, these multitudes (Rev. 15:2) also sing of the fulfillment of all the prophecies, namely, that now all nations should fear God and glorify his name (cf. Hoeksema, 1974:522-526). Israel in the OT already sang the Song of the Lamb, and vice versa, the people of the Lamb in the NT also sing the Song of Moses (cf. Du Rand, 1997:273). Thus, the Song of Moses is the Song of the Lamb. The old and the new dispensations sing the same song, the Song of Moses *and* of the Lamb due to the fulfilled salvation of Christ.

It is clear that the three songs in Revelation 19:1-8 note the fulfilled salvation and the triumphant kingdom of God, in spite of the constant threat of Christ's enemies. The martyrs praise the characteristics of God, namely, his truth and righteousness which are in accordance with his works (Rev. 19:2). Jesus fulfills the role of the Paschal Lamb (Isa. 53:7) and causes the triumphant redeemed to sing 'the Hallel (i.e. Hallelujah) Psalms' (Pss. 113-118, cf. Ex. 15:21; Rev. 19:1, 3, 4, 6). In John's contemporary context, Revelation 19:6 "Hallelujah! The Lord our God the Almighty reigns" is a strong proclamation of God's absolute sovereignty which recalls the punishment of the Egyptian gods (Ex. 12:12; Boring, 1986:257). In short, John's first readers as the New Exodus community must have encouraged by these songs.

3.2. Exodus Theme in Revelation 12-13

Because the Exodus theme is a theological framework to NT authors including John, it is significant to understand Revelation 12-13 in terms of the Exodus motif. John is offering an image to the oppressed Christians in Asia Minor, a symbol derived from the Exodus experience of deliverance and liberation. In particular, John intends to convince his audiences as the community of the New Exodus, of the fact that God's protection leads them to the asylum in Pella via the Jordan River during the Jewish-Roman War (Rev. 12:6, 14).

John associates the dragon (Rev. 12:3) with Egypt and Rome/Jerusalem, since the OT metaphors of the sea monster predominantly portray Egypt as an opponent of God's people (Pss. 74:13-14; 89:10; Hab. 3:8-15), and John sees in Revelation 12 a replay of the Exodus pattern (Beale, 1999:633). When John introduces the appearance of the dragon in heaven, he significantly adds the word 'red' – it is the only instance in the whole Bible where the dragon is mentioned as red. The red dragon is reminiscent of the Red Sea of the OT, indicating to John's audiences that, although the dragon is indeed awesome, God will surely overcome it. Because of the long tradition held by the Jewish people, Jewish audiences would immediately have understood God's impending overthrow of the dragon as soon as John mentioned the great red dragon (Kio, 1989:131). The first historical circumstances of Revelation 12:4 to which the idea corresponds, and in which it is realized, may be found in the effort of Pharaoh to destroy the infant Moses (Miligan, 1889:202).

Revelation 12:6 and 13 describe the woman's flight to the wilderness in clear Exodus terms. The desert (Rev. 12:6, 14) is a common symbol in both OT and NT for a place of God's protection while one waits for the fulfillment of promises. Even the eagle's wings (Rev. 12:14) make patent reference to Exodus 19:4 and Deuteronomy 32:10-12 in which the wings of the eagle are a symbol of God's protection and providence (cf. Mazzaferri, 1989:371). In Revelation 12:14 the combination of the Exodus theme and the re-creation theme is emphasized. White (1989:117-118) correctly articulates the point as follows:

> John's allusion to especially Dt. 32:10-11 is significant, for in the text Moses compares God's presence with Israel in the wilderness to God's presence at creation in Ge. 1:2. That Moses does in fact make this comparison is signaled by two points. On the one hand, the verb used to describe God's activity in Dt. 32:11 (יְרַחֵף) occurs again in the Pentateuch only when Moses describes the Spirit's activity at creation in Ge. 1:2b (מְרַחֶפֶת; LXX: ἐπεφέρετο). On the other hand, the noun used to describe the wilderness where God accompanied Israel in Dt. 32:10 (וּבְתֹהוּ) occurs again in the Pentateuch only when Moses describes the state of the earth over which the Spirit hovered at creation in Ge. 1:2a (תֹהוּ; LXX: ἀόρατος). From these lexical parallels it is not difficult to see that in Dt. 32:10-11 and Ex. 19:4 Moses interprets the Exodus event as a redemptive reenactment of creation, indeed as Israel's redemptive re-creation. When John alludes to those texts in Rev. 12:14, it is no more difficult to see that he understands the woman's experiences as her participation in the new Exodus under the Lamb. ... John is also telling us that the woman's participation in the Messianic Exodus entails her redemptive re-creation.

Apart from the purely metaphorical meaning of God's protection, Exodus 19:4 may be political in nature. In Egypt the goddess Nekhbet is the vulture goddess who represented Upper Egypt and served as a protecting deity for Pharaoh and the land. Nekhbet was depicted as particularly maternal and was believed to assist at royal and divine births. Significant building of her temple in el-Kab took place in the Eighteenth Dynasty toward the end of the Israelite stay in Egypt, so that she was a popular goddess at that time. In Egypt God protected Israel, however. Therefore, Exodus 19:4 and Deuteronomy 32:11 speak of the Lord's care and protection of his people using the imagery that was familiar from Egyptian metaphors of care and protection (Walton & Matthews, 1997:106, 267).

In terms of the Exodus motif the blood (Rev. 12:11) serves as a seal of protection and safety. Blood as a symbol of death binds both God and the people together as one in partnership in the covenant seal (Ex. 19:4-6; 24:3-8; Kio, 1989:134). Although John's clear intertextuality of Exodus cannot be denied, in his doctoral dissertation White (1989:114) points out the difference between the victory in Revelation 12:11 and the victory during Exodus in the OT: "The great irony of Israel's victory over the dragon (Egypt) had been that, though they were released from Egypt, they were not released from their sins. Therefore, through the law given to Israel in their continuing bondage to sin, God could accuse them of sins and by his indictments subject them to the curses of defeat and death. The saint's victory over the dragon is, however, profoundly different. As depicted in Revelation 12:10-11, the holy seed is still accused of sins, but they are accused by the dragon, not God."

Hanson (1993:226) captures the significance of the blood (Rev. 12:11; cf. Rev. 7:14; 19:13) in terms of the purity-uncleanness social system by comparing Revelation with Leviticus: instead of Aaronic priesthood who must manipulate animal blood in a sanctuary, the Lamb's[5] blood accomplished redemption for all and created a new community in which all members are symbolically priests (Rev. 5:9-10; 7:14). The image of the blood of the Lamb also reverses the categorization of blood on garments in Leviticus 6:27. Instead of polluting, the Lamb's blood becomes a

---

[5] Here, the idea of a lamb offered as a cultic sacrifice certainly contributes to this imagery. One should not too quickly interpret the lamb image as solely, or even primarily, cultic-sacrificial terminology (see Reddish, 1995:215).

metaphor of purification when the saints and the Word of God wash their robes in it (Rev. 19:13-14; cf. Lev. 7:14; 19:13).

Embedded in the Exodus motif, John also uses 'the eagle metaphor' (Rev. 12:14), which was familiar to his audience in Asia Minor as a symbol of the Roman army, in order to accentuate the fact that it is not Rome but God who protects the seven churches in Asia Minor. As Sweet (1990:203) notes, the model for her flight (Rev. 12:14) is the Exodus story. God brought his people on eagle's wings into the wilderness (Ex. 19:4 [LXX: αὐτοὶ ἑωράκατε ὅσα πεποίηκα τοῖς Αἰγυπτίοις καὶ ἀνέλαβον ὑμᾶς ὡσεὶ ἐπὶ πτερύγων ἀετῶν καὶ προσηγαγόμην ὑμᾶς πρὸς ἐμαυτόν⁶ – eagles' wings]; Dt. 32:11 [LXX: ὡς ἀετὸς σκεπάσαι⁷ ... τὰς πτέρυγας αὐτοῦ – eagle's wings like Rev. 12:14], where they were nourished for forty-two years. The river-flood (Rev. 12:15) evokes Pharaoh's attempt to destroy male Israelites in the river (Ex. 1:22) and his pursuit of Israel between the waters of the Red Sea (Ex. 14:21; cf. Beale & McDonough, 2007:1126).

Revelation 12:16 may be linked to Exodus 15:12 (נָטִיתָ יְמִינְךָ תִּבְלָעֵמוֹ אָרֶץ:); LXX: ἐξέτεινας τὴν δεξιάν σου κατέπιεν αὐτοὺς γῆ ⁸ You stretched forth your right hand, the earth

---

⁶ Instead of the second person plural pronoun of MT, the translators of LXX use αὐτοί. This is short for ὑμεῖς αὐτοι, but should be translated emphatically: 'you yourselves'. Both ἑωράκατε and the verb in the subordinate clause πεποίηκα are in the perfect, thus 'You have seen what I have done'; the latter verb (ἀνέλαβον) appears as an aorist which makes good sense as a simple past. Israel has taken note not only of the salvific acts, ὅσα πεποίηκα but also of God's bringing them as on eagles' wings, i.e. soaring with ease, provident and protective to himself at Sinai, where the covenant between God and his people is formally enacted (see Wevers, 1990:293-294).

⁷ LXX presents a somewhat different picture from that of MT. Instead of an eagle יָעִיר ('arouses, awakes'), LXX has σκεπάσαι. As to John, to the translator it was God's constant watch over his people that was intended, and the change is obviously an attempt to make the figure fit the notion of divine providence (Wevers, 1995:515).

⁸ The second line of Ex. 15:12 appears asyndetically in portraying the effect of the first line. Some add καὶ to introduce the line. Similarly some readings

swallowed them up), in which 'the earth' drank the enemies who were pursuing the fleeing Israelites (Minear, 1991:76). The earth opening its mouth (Rev. 12:16: καὶ ἤνοιξεν ἡ γῆ τὸ στόμα αὐτῆς, καὶ κατέπιεν) also calls to mind the destruction of Korah in Deuteronomy 11:6 (ἀνοίξασα ἡ γῆ τὸ στόμα αὐτῆς κατέπιεν αὐτοὺς; cf. Ge. 4:1-16; Nu. 16:30-33). If so, the earth's protection of the woman in Revelation 12:16 ironically reverses the earth's endangerment of the remaining Israelites in Numbers 16:34 and Deuteronomy 11:6. Although John freely uses and changes the Exodus, the results of the new Exodus are the same as the old: the mother of the seed, as it were, walks on dry land through the midst of the waters (Ex. 15:19; cf. White, 1989:118).

As John records the dragon's rage over the woman's escape and his departure from her to wage war against the rest of her seed in Revelation 12:17, he offers this characterization of the seed whom the dragon would overcome: 'who keep the authoritative instruction of God and hold to the testimony of Jesus' (cf. Rev. 14:12). The phrase 'obey God's commandments' has a theological intertextuality with Exodus. In the time of the Exodus, Israel's obeying of God's commandments would have constituted her victory over sin, the sequel to which would have been her re-creation as God's holy kingdom (cf. Rev. 1:5-6). The phrase describing the seed's keeping of God's authoritative instruction (i.e. commandments) in Revelation 12:17 means the seed's re-creation as the kingdom being constituted by the Lamb. In fact, John's audience's salvation surpasses that of Israel: unlike Israel, they have been constituted as God's kingdom not simply by divine precept, but by divine power as well (White, 1989:120-121).

It is possible to conjecture that Revelation 13:3-4 shows a parody of Exodus 15:11 in that the beast's victory over death is paralleled with God's victory over the Egyptians (Kraft, 1974:272). The dragon's sending of the two beasts (Rev. 13:1, 11)

---

articulate γῆ as a stylistic improvement, since the unarticulated is a slavish imitation of MT's אֶרֶץ (Wevers, 1990:232).

corresponds with the test at the hands of Balak and Balaam,[9] which Israel encountered upon their entry into the Promised Land (Sweet, 1990:203). The rhetorical question, "Who is like the beast?" in Revelation 13:4 is an echo of language frequently used in praising God (e.g. Exodus 15:11: LXX: τίς ὅμοιός σοι ἐν θεοῖς κύριε τίς ὅμοιός σοι δεδοξασμένος ἐν ἁγίοις θαυμαστὸς ἐν δόξαις ποιῶν τέρατα;[10] Psalms 35:10; 113:5; Beckwith, 1967:636). Following the rhetorical question "who is like the beast, and who is able to wage war against him?", a series of three aspects of Yahweh's incomparability is raised in a further rhetorical question: his magnificent holiness, his praiseworthy deeds, and his extraordinary accomplishment. Thus, John reminds his audiences of the strong

---

[9] In the OT, in only two cases (Ge. 3:1-5; Nu. 22:22-35) are animals endowed with the capacity to express themselves articulately, and here too the impact of their speech is central to the understanding of these texts. A number of significant intertextual parallels among Ge. 3:1-5, Nu. 22:22-35, and Rev. 13 reveal John's Exodus intertextuality in connection with Genesis. Although there are partial parallels, the outstanding parallels are: (1) the ass, the snake, and the beast use interrogatory statements to persuade the listener, but their questions have different rhetorical intent (Ge. 3:4-5; Nu. 22:28; cf. Rev. 13:4); (2) the image of an angel armed with a sword is common to the three stories (Ge. 3:24; Nu. 22:31; cf. Rev. 13:10); (3) the motif of knowledge/wisdom is also common (Ge. 3:6; Nu. 23:34; Rev. 13:18); (4) obedience to the voice of the snake and the beast entails the rejection of divine authority; (5) evil is associated with a foreign ruler in the story of Numbers and Revelation; (6) the animals speak only by divine initiative (e.g. the divine passive in Rev. 13), and have no special powers of their own; (7) in the three texts it seems that the animals exhibit a deeper understanding of the relationship between the human and the divine than their human counterparts; (8) the three animals lead people astray, the snake and the beast figuratively and the ass literally; and (9) the significance of cursing in the three texts is noteworthy (Ge. 3:14-19; Nu. 22:17; Rev. 13:6) The intertextual relationship among the stories of the anomalous animal speech sheds light on larger patterns of inner-biblical interpretation (see Savran, 1994:34, 55).

[10] These hymnodic lines are nominal clauses, with attributive modifiers emphasizing the point of comparison in the question 'who is like you'. The first instance is modified simply by a prepositional phrase ἐν θεοῖς. This in turn influences the ἐν phrase, which follows in the next line, i.e. ἐν ἁγίοις, where MT has a singular word בַּקֹּדֶשׁ 'holiness'. This might then be translated 'among the holy ones', presumably taken as parallel to ἐν θεοῖς (Wevers, 1990:231).

contrast between the true God and the beast and that they are forced to remain faithful to the incomparable God.

The temple motif is also important for the Exodus theme in Revelation 13:6. The fellowship and residence of God in the tabernacle in the historical Exodus event (Ex. 40:34) foreshadow God's dwelling (τὴν σκηνὴν αὐτοῦ) and fellowship in the true temple, believers who experience the New Exodus in Christ (cf. Rev. 21:3). The Exodus by Moses is not only a type of the New Exodus by Christ but is also a type of the deliverance from the Exile. So, the Exodus by Jesus is the archetype of the future consummated salvation of God, as well as the antitype of the Exodus by Moses.

The fact that for the word 'slain' John uses the Greek word ἐσφαγμένου in Revelation 13:8 (also Rev. 5:6, 9, 12) shows another Exodus theme. Since σφάζω refers to the violent death of the lamb slaughtered for sacrifice (Ex. 12:6), the image evokes the memory of Israel's Exodus and liberation from Egypt, which was considered in Judaism as a prototype of the final eschatological salvation (Kio, 1989:132-133).

The mark in Revelation 13:17 (cf. Rev. 14:9b) indicating that the people belong to the beast has the same meaning as the sign in Exodus 13:9, 16. Both mean the mark of possession (Kio, 1989:126). In connection with the mark, another feature from Exodus appears: the first plague of the seven bowls in Revelation 16:2 is 'an ugly and painful sore' on those who had the mark of the beast and worshipped his image (cf. Ex. 9:9-11).

Relying on the Exodus-based intertextual theme, John is offering an image to the oppressed Christians in Asia Minor, a symbol derived from the Exodus experience of deliverance and liberation. In order to accomplish his goal, John used a number of Exodus symbols and images. He did this not for the sake of secrecy but for the sake of impact – they have a great evocative and emotive power (Kio, 1989:131). In particular, John uses the battle between God and the dragon of Egypt to interpret Christ's inaugural victory over the dragon which makes war against the Church. John intends to convince his audiences as the community of the New Exodus of the fact that God's protection leads them to the asylum in Pella via the Jordan River during the Jewish-Roman War (cf. Kraft, 1974:264). The Exodus intertextuality is so closely intertwined with the re-creation motif that John clearly accentuates the surpassing status of his audience (as the recreated new Exodus community) to that of the Israel in the OT. If Revelation 12-13 is read from the Exodus intertexts, the Exodus intertextuality functions as a paradigm to describe God's saving of his own people as well as his judgment of the oppressors (cf. Du Rand, 1996:52-53). The eschatological redemption in terms of the Exodus theme for which Christ has worked is so clear in Revelation 12-13 that God's people in Asia Minor, who have already experienced his/her salvation but still anticipate its consummation,[11] have to praise God with great joy.

In summary, when John makes use of the Exodus theme he sometimes changes its expression and thought in terms of the archetypal Exodus of Christ in order to make his message proper to his audience. In this sense, John understands that the Exodus is not so much 'Christocentric' as 'Christotelic', in which the person and works of Christ plays the role of a starting point to understand OT and NT texts.

Conclusion

The Exodus in Moses' time plays both an antitype for pre-Exodus period and a type for post-Exodus. Although the Exodus theme begins with the Exodus from Egypt in full scale, the cross and resurrection of Christ, the new Moses, plays the crucial role of archetype for all Exodus events in the progressive redemptive

---

[11] The story of salvation, the new exodus, ends at Revelation 21:8 with its depiction of the new creation. The description of the bride of the Lamb is given deliberate contrast to the antichristian city described in Revelation 17. For this reason, the Book of Revelation reaches its climax as the story of the harlot and the bride. It is in truth a tale of two cities (Beasley-Murrey, 1997:1031).

history. Jesus' Exodus from Jerusalem (Lk. 9:31) plays the crucial role of type for the consummated Exodus of the New Covenantal people by his Parousia in the final stage of redemptive history. Revelation 12-13 expresses the fulfillment of Exodus and foretastes its consummation on the basis of Jesus' archetypal Exodus. The seven churches in Asia Minor as a new Exodus and recreated community must have experienced the new and eschatological Exodus from the Roman and the apostate Jewish persecuting power.

Bibliography

AUNE, D.E. 1998. *Revelation 6-16: Word Biblical Commentary. 52B.* Nashville : Thomas Nelson Publishers.

BEALE, G.K. 1999. *The Book of Revelation.* NIGTC. Grand Rapids : Eerdmans.

BEALE, G.K. & MCDONOUGH, S.M. 2007. *Revelation.* (*In* Beale, G.K. & Carson, D.A. eds. *Commentary on the New Testament use of the Old Testament.* Grand Rapids : Baker Academic. p. 1081-1161.)

BEASLEY-MURRAY, G.R. 1997. *Book of Revelation.* (*In* Martin, R.P. & Davids P.H. eds. *Dictionary of the Later New Testament and Its Developments.* Downers Grove : IVP. p. 1025-1038.)

BECKWITH, I.T. 1967. *The Apocalypse of John: Studies in Introduction with a Critical and Exegetical Commentary.* Grand Rapids : Baker.

BORING, M.E. 1986. "The Theology of Revelation: The Lord Our God the Almighty Reigns." *Interpretation*, 40(3):257-269.

BROYLES, C.C. 1992. "Moses." (*In* Green, J.B., McKnight, S., and Marshall, I.H., eds. *Dictionary of Jesus and the Gospels.* Leicester : Inter-Varsity Press. p. 560-562.)

CHEVALIER, J.M. 1997. *A Postmodern Revelation: Signs of Astrology and the Apocalypse.* Toronto: University of Toronto Press.

COLLINS, J.J. 1995. "The Exodus and Biblical Theology." *Biblical Theology Bulletin*, 25(4):152-160.

DAUBE, D. 1979. *The Exodus Pattern in the Bible*. Westport : Greenwood Press.

DILLARD, R.B. & LONGMAN III, T. 1994. *An Introduction to the Old Testament*. Grand Rapids : Zondervan.

DU RAND, J.A. 1993. "A 'Basso Ostinato' in the Structuring of the Apocalypse of John?" *Neotestamentica*, 27(2):299-311.

DU RAND, J.A. 1996. " '... Let him hear what the Spirit says ...': The Functional Role and Theological Meaning of the Spirit in the Book of Revelation." *Ex Auditu*, 12:43-58.

DU RAND, J.A. 1997. *Johannine Perspectives. Part 1: Introduction to the Johannine Writings*. Johannesburg : Orion Publishers.

FRETHEIM, T.E. 1991. "The Plagues as Ecological Signs of Historical Disaster." *Journal of Biblical Literature*, 110(3):385-396.

GARRETT, S.R. 1990. "Exodus from Bondage: Luke 9:31 and Acts 12:1-24." *Catholic Biblical Quarterly*, 52(4): 656-680.

GOLDSWORTHY, G. 1991. *According to Plan*. Seoul: Korea Scripture Union.

HANSON, K.C. 1993. "Blood and Purity in Leviticus and Revelation." *Listening*, 28(3):215-230.

HOEKSEMA, H. 1974. *Behold, He Comes: An Exposition of the Book of Revelation*. Grand Rapids: Reformed Free Publishing Association.

JENKINS, F. 1972. *The Old Testament in the Book of Revelation*. Marion: Cogdill Foundation Publications.

JORDAN, J.B. 1996. *Esther: Historical & Chronological Comments (II). Biblical Chronology*, 8(4):1-4.

KARIAMADAM, P. 1997. "Transfiguration and Jesus' Ascended Glory." *Bible Bhashyam*, 23(1):1-13.

KIO, S.H. 1989. "The Exodus Symbol of Liberation in the Apocalypse and Its Relevance for Some Aspects of Translation." *Bible Translator*, 40:120-135.

KRAFT, H. 1974. *Die Offenbarung des Johannes*. Tübingen : Mohr-Siebeck.

KIM, S.Y. 1997. *Kingdom of God*. (*In* Martin, R.P. & Davids, P.H., *eds. Dictionary of the Later New Testament and Its Developments*. Leicester : Inter-Varsity Press. p. 629-638.)

MAZZAFERRI, F.D. 1989. *The Genre of the Book of Revelation from a Source-Critical Perspective*. Berlin: Walter de Gruyter.

MILIGAN, W. 1889. *The Book of Revelation*. London: Hodder and Stoughton.

MINEAR, P.S. 1991. "Far as the Curse is Found: The Point of Revelation 12:15-16." *Novum Testamentum*, XXXIII (1):71-77.

MOUNCE, R.H. 1983. *The Book of Revelation*. Grand Rapids: Eerdmans.

REDDISH, M.G. 1995. "Martyr Christology in the Apocalypse." (*In* Porter, S.E. & Evans, C.A., *eds. The Johannine Writings: a Sheffield Reader*. Sheffield : Sheffield Academic Press. p. 212-222.)

SAVRAN, G. 1994. "Beastly Speech: Intertextuality, Balaam's Ass and the Garden of Eden." *Journal for the Study of the Old Testament*, 64:33-55.

SWEET, J.P.M. 1990. *Revelation*. London: SCM.

WALTON, J.H. & MATTHEWS, V.H. 1997. *The IVP Bible Background Commentary: Genesis-Deuteronomy*. Downers Grove : IVP.

WEVERS, J.W. 1990. *Notes on the Greek Text of Exodus*. Atlanta : Scholars Press.

WEVERS, J.W. 1995. *Notes on the Greek Text of Deuteronomy*. Atlanta : Scholars Press.

WHITE, R.F. 1989. "Victory and House Building in Revelation 20:1-21:8: A Thematic Study." Ann Arbor : UMI.

"בְּבֵיתִי in 1 Chr 17:14: Temple or Kingdom?"[1]

Sunwoo Hwang

As the counterpart to Nathan's oracle of the Davidic dynastic promise in 2 Sam 7, 1 Chr 17 is a key text for the understanding the Chronicler's view on the Davidic dynastic promise. In particular, verse 14 is a focal point.

וְהַעֲמַדְתִּיהוּ בְּבֵיתִי וּבְמַלְכוּתִי עַד־הָעוֹלָם וְכִסְאוֹ
יִהְיֶה נָכוֹן עַד־עוֹלָם

"And I shall establish him in my house and my kingdom forever and his throne shall be established forever."

2 Sam 17:16 reads as follows:

וְנֶאְמַן בֵּיתְךָ וּמַמְלַכְתְּךָ עַד־עוֹלָם לְפָנֶיךָ כִּסְאֲךָ
יִהְיֶה נָכוֹן עַד־עוֹלָם

"Your house and your kingdom shall be made firm forever before you; your throne shall be established forever."

'Your (David's) house and your kingdom' of 2 Sam 17:16 is changed to 'my (YWHW's) house and my kingdom' in 1 Chr 17:14, and 'your throne' of 2 Sam 17:16 is changed to 'his (Solomon's) throne' in 1 Chr 17:14. The identification of בְּבֵיתִי

---

[1] This academic paper was presented at the Historical Books (Old Testament) section of the 2008 International Society of Biblical Literature conference in Auckland, New Zealand.

"בְּבֵיתִי in 1 Chr 17:14: Temple or Kingdom?"

in 1 Chr 17:14 is pivotal in the discussion of the Chronicler's view on the Davidic royal promise. If it is rendered as the temple, the house of YWHW, it can buttress the position that the Davidic royal promise is realized through the temple and its cultus. This position stands with Wilhelm Rudolpf's claim:

> The failure of the Davidic dynasty could be borne so long as the second pillar of the theocracy, the Jerusalem temple is stood firm.[2]

The LXX's rendering on the two verses is different from that of the MT.

> καὶ πιστωθήσεται ὁ οἶκος αὐτοῦ καὶ ἡ βασιλεία αὐτοῦ ἕως αἰῶνος ἐνώπιον ἐμοῦ καὶ ὁ θρόνος αὐτοῦ ἔσται ἀνωρθωμένος εἰς τὸν αἰῶνα (2 Sam 7:16).

> "And his house and his kingdom shall be made firm forever before me and his throne shall be restored forever."

> καὶ πιστώσω αὐτὸν ἐν οἴκῳ μου καὶ ἐν βασιλείᾳ αὐτοῦ ἕως αἰῶνος καὶ ὁ θρόνος αὐτοῦ ἔσται ἀνωρθωμένος ἕως αἰῶνος (1 Chr 17:14).

> "And I shall establish him in my house and in his kingdom forever and his throne shall be restored forever."

It is noticed that the focus is moved from David to Solomon in 2 Sam 17:16 of the LXX by changing the suffix: 'your house and your kingdom...your throne' to 'his house and his kingdom... and his throne.' In 1 Chr 17:14 of the LXX, the first person suffix of the MT is changed to the third person: 'my kingdom' to 'his kingdom.'

W. E. Lemke's chart is helpful to the difference.[3]

---

[2] Wilhelm Rudolph, "Problems of the Books of Chronicles," *Vetus Testamentum* 4 (1954), 404.

	1. House	2. Kingdom	3. Throne	Referring to whom?
2 Sam 17:16 (MT)	your	your	your	David
2 Sam 17:16 (LXX)	his	his	his	Solomon
1 Chr 17:14 (MT)	my	my	his	Yahweh (1 and 2) Solomon (3)
1 Chr 17:14 (LXX)	my	his	his	Yahweh (1) Solomon (2 and 3)

Although it is difficult to explain all the variations of the suffixes, at least there is a noticeable change in Chronicles; God will establish him (Solomon) in the House of God.

Concerning the identification of בְּבֵיתִי, let us first examine the use of בית in 1 Chr 17. There are fourteen occurrences of בית in 1 Chr 17. Except for the בית in verse 14, the meanings of the other 13 occurrences are clear: palace (v. 1a, 1c), temple (vv. 4, 5, 6, 12), dynasty (vv. 10, 16, 17, 23, 24, 25, 27).

Steven L. McKenzie argues that the parallel structure of verse 14, 'my house and my kingdom' leads us to understand בְּבֵיתִי as 'in God's dynasty.'[4] Mckenzie views the structure of the phrase as tautological. From the phrase, בְּבֵיתִי וּבְמַלְכוּתִי, H. G. M. Williamson claims that God is the real king of Israel, his kingdom.[5] Namely, 'my house' refers to God's kingdom of Israel.

---

[3] W. E. Lemke, "Synoptic Studies in the Chronicler's History" (Th. D. diss., Harvard University, 1963), 43.
[4] Steven L. McKenzie, *1-2 Chronicles*, Abingdon Old Testament Commentaries (Nashville: Abingdon Press, 2004), 158.
[5] H. G. M. Williamson, *1 and 2 Chronicles*, The New Century Bible Commentary (Grand Rapids: Eerdmans, 1982), 136.

"בְּבֵיתִי" in 1 Chr 17:14: Temple or Kingdom?"

To defend YWHW's kingship over Israel, Williamson cites other passages of Chronicles[6]:

1 Chr 28:5 וּמִכָּל־בָּנַי כִּי רַבִּים בָּנִים נָתַן לִי יְהוָה
וַיִּבְחַר בִּשְׁלֹמֹה בְנִי לָשֶׁבֶת עַל־כִּסֵּא מַלְכוּת יְהוָה
עַל־יִשְׂרָאֵל

"And of all my sons, for YHWH has given me many sons, he has chosen Solomon, my son to sit on the throne of the kingdom of YHWH over Israel" (1 Chr 28:5).

1 Chr 29:11 לְךָ יְהוָה הַגְּדֻלָּה וְהַגְּבוּרָה וְהַתִּפְאֶרֶת
וְהַנֵּצַח וְהַהוֹד כִּי־כֹל בַּשָּׁמַיִם וּבָאָרֶץ לְךָ יְהוָה הַמַּמְלָכָה
וְהַמִּתְנַשֵּׂא לְכֹל לְרֹאשׁ

"For you, YHWH, is the greatness, the power, the glory, the perpetuity, and the majesty; for all that is in the heavens and on the earth for you YHWH, the kingdom, you are exalted as head over all" (1 Chr 29:11).

1 Chr 29:23 וַיֵּשֶׁב שְׁלֹמֹה עַל־כִּסֵּא יְהוָה לְמֶלֶךְ
תַּחַת־דָּוִיד אָבִיו וַיַּצְלַח וַיִּשְׁמְעוּ אֵלָיו כָּל־יִשְׂרָאֵל

"And Solomon sat on the throne of YHWH, as king instead of David, his father and he prospered, and all Israel obeyed him" (1 Chr 29:23).

2 Chr 9:8 יְהִי יְהוָה אֱלֹהֶיךָ בָּרוּךְ אֲשֶׁר חָפֵץ בְּךָ
לְתִתְּךָ עַל־כִּסְאוֹ לְמֶלֶךְ לַיהוָה אֱלֹהֶיךָ בְּאַהֲבַת אֱלֹהֶיךָ
אֶת־יִשְׂרָאֵל לְהַעֲמִידוֹ לְעוֹלָם וַיִּתֶּנְךָ עֲלֵיהֶם לְמֶלֶךְ לַעֲשׂוֹת
מִשְׁפָּט וּצְדָקָה

---

[6] Ibid.

"Blessed be YHWH your God, who has delighted in you and set you on his throne as king for YHWH your God. Because your God loved Israel establishing them forever, he has made you king over them to do justice and righteousness" (2 Chr 9:8).

2 Chr 13:8 וְעַתָּה אַתֶּם אֹמְרִים לְהִתְחַזֵּק לִפְנֵי
מַמְלֶכֶת יְהוָה בְּיַד בְּנֵי דָוִיד וְאַתֶּם הָמוֹן רָב וְעִמָּכֶם עֶגְלֵי
זָהָב אֲשֶׁר עָשָׂה לָכֶם יָרָבְעָם לֵאלֹהִים

"And now you say that you withstand the kingdom of YHWH in the hand of the sons of David, because you are a great multitude and have with you the golden calves that Jeroboam made as gods for you" (2 Chr 13:8).

Thus, for both McKenzie and Williamson, 'my house' does not mean the temple but the kingdom of Israel, which is God's dynasty. In this interpretation, God's house is bigger than the temple. God's house is expanded to the kingdom of Israel.

However, textual evidence does not support this expanded interpretation of 'God's house.' As we examined in 1 Chr 17, which is a section of the dynastic oracle for David and David's prayer, the other four occurrences of God's בית (vv. 4, 5, 6, 12) designate the temple of God.

Let us examine more closely the book of Chronicles if בית is ever used to designate the kingdom of Israel as the expanded house of God. The following is the examination of the use of the 329 occurrences of בית in Chronicles.

Of the 329 times of all the occurrences of בית in Chronicles it is observed that בית is used variously in each context. Based on the examination, we can categorize the 328 occurrences (except for 1 Chr 17:14) of בית into 14 groups: The Temple of Yahweh, clan, palace, dynasty, house, family, temple of other gods, room, storehouse, home, inside, factory, tabernacle, prison.

"בְּבֵיתִי in 1 Chr 17:14: Temple or Kingdom?"

Usage (328)	Reference
Temple of Yahweh (208)	**1 Chr** 5:36 6:16, 17, 33 9:11, 13, 23a, 26, 27 17:4, 5, 6, 12 22:1, 2, 5, 6, 7, 8, 10, 11, 14, 19 23:4, 24b, 28a, 28b, 32 24:19 25:6a, 6b 26:12, 20, 22, 27 28:2, 3, 6, 10, 12a, 12b, 13a, 13b, 20, 21 29:2, 3a, 3b, 3c, 4, 7, 8, 16 **2 Chr** 1:18a 2: 3, 4, 5a, 5b, 8, 11a 3:1, 3, 4, 5, 6, 7, 8b, 11, 12, 15 4:11, 16, 19, 22a, 22b 5:1a 1b, 7, 13a, 13b, 14 6:2, 5, 7, 8, 9a, 9b, 10, 18, 20, 22, 24, 29, 32, 33, 34, 38 7:1, 2a, 2b, 3, 5, 7, 11a, 11c, 12, 16, 20, 21a, 21b 8:1a, 16a, 16b 9:4, 11a 12:9a, 11 15:18 16:2a 20:5, 9a, 9b, 28 22:12 23:3, 5b, 6, 7, 9, 10a, 10b, 10c, 12, 14b, 18a, 18b, 19, 20a 24:4, 5, 7a, 7b, 8, 12a, 12b, 12c, 13, 14a, 14b, 16, 18, 21, 27 25:24a 26:19, 21b

	27:3 28:21a, 24a, 24b, 24c 29:3, 5, 15, 16a, 16b, 17, 18, 20, 25, 31, 35 30:1, 15 31:10b, 11, 13, 16, 21 33:4, 5, 7a, 7b, 15a, 15b 34:8a, 8b, 9, 10a, 10b, 10c, 14, 15, 17, 30a, 30b 35:2, 3, 8, 20 36:7, 10, 14, 17, 18a, 18b, 19, 23
Clan (40)	**1 Chr** 2:55 4:38 5:13, 15, 24a, 24b 7:2, 4, 7, 9, 40 9:9, 13a, 19 12:29, 31 21:17 23:11, 24a 24:4a, 4b, 6, 30 26:6, 13 28:4a, 4b, 4c **2 Chr** 10:16 11:1 17:14 19:11 22: 10 25:5, 31:10a, 17 35:4, 5a, 5b, 12
Palace (27)	**1 Chr** 14:1 15:1 17:1a, 1c

"בְּבֵיתִי in 1 Chr 17:14: Temple or Kingdom?"

	2 Chr 1:18b 2: 2, 11b 7:11b, 11d 8:1b, 11b 9:3, 11b 12:9b, 10 16:2b 19:1 21:17 23:5a, 15, 20b 25:24b 26:21c 28:7, 21b 33:20, 24
Dynasty (19)	**1 Chr** 12:30 17:10, 16, 17, 23, 24, 25, 27 **2 Chr** 10:19 21:6, 7, 13a, 13b 22:3, 4, 7, 8, 9 35:21
House (7)	**1 Chr** 13:7, 13, 14b 15:25 **2 Chr** 8:11a 26:21a 34:11
Family (5)	**1 Chr** 7:23 10:6 13:14a, 14c

	16:43b
Temple of other gods (4)	**1 Chr** 10:10a, 10b **2 Chr** 23:17 32:21
Room (Nave) (4)	**1 Chr** 28:11 **2 Chr** 3:8a, 10, 13
Storehouse (5)	**1 Chr** 26:15 28:11 **2 Chr** 9:16 9:20 16:10
Home (4)	**1 Chr** 16:43a **2 Chr** 11:4 18:16 25:19
Inside (2)	**2 Chr** 4:4 23:14a
Factory (1)	**1 Chr** 4:21
Tabernacle (1)	**1 Chr** 9:23b

"בְּבֵיתִי in 1 Chr 17:14: Temple or Kingdom?"

Prison (1)	**2 Chr** 18:26

The above analysis of בית betrays that the 328 occurrences, other than 1 Chr 17:14, there is not a single use of בית to refer to the kingdom of Israel. This exhaustive analysis tell us that it is highly unlikely that the בית in 1 Chr 17:14 means the kingdom of Israel as the expanded house of God.

The cited passages by Williamson (1 Chr 28:5; 29:11, 23; 2 Chr 9:8; 13:8) witness Yahweh's lordship over Israel; the real king of Israel is Yahweh. This phrase corresponds well to וּבְמַלְכוּתִי (and my kingdom) of 1 Chr 17:14. However, it is not persuasive to connect the cited passages to בְּבֵיתִי (in my house). In fact, 'Yahweh's בית' does not occur in the cited passages at all. Yahweh's lordship over Israel is vindicated by the phrases '(Yahweh's) kingdom' and '(Yahweh's) throne.'

To answer McKenzie's point, the parallel structure 'my house and my kingdom,' does not suffice to show that 'my house' refers to the kingdom of Israel. Mckenzie does not explain why the parallel structure is to be understood as tautological. In the parallel structure, it is not necessary that the first word is semantically limited or defined by the second word. Thus, as the other occurrences of God's בית of 1 Chr 17, it is most appropriate to understand בְּבֵיתִי in 1 Chr 17:14 as 'in the temple of God.'

The next inquiry to investigate is the meaning of the phrase of 1 Chr 17:14:

וְהַעֲמַדְתִּיהוּ בְּבֵיתִי וּבְמַלְכוּתִי

"And I shall establish him in my house and my kingdom"

Since the interpretation of בְּבֵיתִי takes the most vital place for this investigation, let us first examine the use of the proposition ב particularly with בית. 'בבית' occurs 40 times with various prefixes and suffixes in the book of Chronicles: בבית(31), בביתו(4), בביתי(1), בביתך(1), ובבית(2), ובביתו(1). The following chart is the examination of 40 times of 'בבית' in Chronicles.

Reference	Use of ב
1 Chr	
5:36	In
7:23	In
13:14	In
17:1a, 1b, 5, 14	In, ?(14)
21:17	In
26:12	In
28:4	In
29:3	In

"בְּבֵיתִי in 1 Chr 17:14: Temple or Kingdom?"

Reference	Use of בְּ
2 Chr	
3:10	In
4:11	In
6:22, 24	In
7:11a, 11b	In
8:11	In
9:16	In
10:19	Against
20:5, 9	In
22:12	In
23:3, 5	In
24:14	Against
25:19, 24	In
26:19	In
31:11	In
33:4, 7a, 7b, 24	In
34:10a, 10b, 15, 17	In
35:3	In
36:17	In

As the examination of the use of בְּ with בית shows, out of 40 times of בְּ with בית, 37 times of בְּ with בית are used as a spatial 'in,' and 2 times of בְּ with בית are in the sense of adversative 'against,' and בְּ with בית of 1 Chr 17:14 is our concern. The outcome of the examination indicates that the use of בְּ with בית in Chronicles is not variant, and the dominant use of בְּ with בית is spatial 'in.' Since there is no idiosyncratic use of בְּ with בית discovered in Chronicles, and it is most natural to apply the spatial 'in' for the בְּ with בַּיִת in the context of 1 Chr 17:14, the most appropriate translation of בְּבֵיתִי is 'in my house' which is 'in the temple of God.'

If the בְּבֵיתִי is rendered as 'in the temple of God,' we can rephrase the sentence:

'And I shall establish him in the temple and in my kingdom.'

Since the third suffix is clearly Solomon, we can apply this sentence to the scene of Solomon's coronation in 1 Chr 29:21-25.

> On the next day they offered sacrifices and burnt offerings to the LORD, a thousand bulls, a thousand rams, and a thousand lambs, with their libations, and sacrifices in abundance for all Israel; and they ate and drank before the LORD on that day with great joy. They made David's son Solomon king a second time; they anointed him as the LORD's prince, and Zadok as priest. Then Solomon sat on the throne of the LORD, succeeding his father David as king; he prospered, and all Israel obeyed him. All the leaders and the mighty warriors, and also all the sons of King David, pledged their allegiance to King Solomon. The LORD highly exalted Solomon in the sight of all Israel, and bestowed upon him such royal majesty as had not been on any king before him in Israel. (1 Chr 29:21-25, NRSV)

In 1 Chr 29:22, though there is שֵׁנִית (second time) in the MT, some other texts (e.g., LXX[B]) omit שֵׁנִית. Whether that is the first or second coronation feast, it took place before Solomon's building of the temple. Simply because there was no temple building yet, it is not possible to apply the phrase, 'And I shall establish him in the temple,' into the scene of Solomon's coronation.

William M. Schniedewind makes an attempt to specify the meaning of the phrase:

> The meaning of 'my house and my kingdom' (ובמלכותי בביתי) is amply clear when the Chronicler reuses this language to refer to Solomon's temple and palace. In 2 Chr 1:18, we are

"בְּבֵיתִי in 1 Chr 17:14: Temple or Kingdom?"

told that Solomon resolved to build 'a house for the name of YWHW and a house for his kingdom' (יהוה ובית למלכותו בית לשם). In 2 Chr 2:11, Hiram praises Solomon who has the wisdom to build 'a house for YWHW and a house for his kingdom' (בית ליהוה ובית למלכותו). This pairing of the house of God and the house of the kingdom, that is the temple and the palace, relies on the Chronicler's version of the Dynastic Oracle in 1 Chr 17:14...[7]

Schniedewind draws 2 Chr 1:18 and 2:11 for the interpretation of the phrase in 1 Chr 17:14. By relying on the two passages, 2 Chr 1:18 and 2:11, he interprets the phrase, 'in my house and my kingdom' as 'in the temple and the palace.' However, his connection of the two passages to the 1 Chr 17:14 phrase fails when we notice that ובמלכותי (and in my kingdom) of 1 Chr 17:14 is different from ובית למלכותו (and the house of his kingdom) of the two 2 Chr phrases. ובית למלכותו of the two 2 Chr passages means 'the palace' as Schniedwind says, but ובמלכותי of the 1 Chr 17:14 does not mean 'the palace.' מלכות is a late biblical Hebrew word, which means 'dominion,' 'kingdom,' or 'kingship.'[8]

As Gary Knoppers avers, it is most appropriate to interpret the phrase וְהַעֲמַדְתִּיהוּ בְּבֵיתִי as an indication of a special tie between the temple and David's heir.[9] Through the book of Chronicles, the kings of the Davidic dynasty play important roles in the temple. Not only does the Chronicler describe David and Solomon as the preparer and completer of the building of the

---

[7] William M. Schniedewind, "King and Priest in the Book of Chronicles and the Duality of Qumran Messianism," *Journal of Jewish Studies* 45 (1994), 73.

[8] Philip J. Nel, "מלך," *New International Dictionary of Old Testament Theology & Exegesis* II, ed., Willem A. VanGemeren (Grand Rapids: Zondervan, 1997), 957-958.

[9] Gary N. Knoppers, *1 Chronicles 10-29*, Anchor Bible (New York: Doubleday, 2004), 672-673.

temple, but the kings of the Davidic dynasty appoint and assemble temple personnel for various roles such as priests, singers, gatekeepers, and treasurers (e.g., 1 Chr 23-26; 2 Chr 29:4), provide offerings (e.g., 2 Chr 30:24; 35:7), repair the temple (e.g., 2 Chr 24:4-5; 29:3). To explicate the intriguing phrase בְּבֵיתִי וְהַעֲמַדְתִּיהוּ, 2 Chr 31:21 supplies an important clue:

וּבְכָל־מַעֲשֶׂה אֲשֶׁר־הֵחֵל בַּעֲבוֹדַת בֵּית־הָאֱלֹהִים וּבַתּוֹרָה וּבַמִּצְוָה לִדְרֹשׁ לֵאלֹהָיו בְּכָל־לְבָבוֹ עָשָׂה וְהִצְלִיחַ

"And every work that he began in the service of the house of God, and in the law and in the commandment to seek his God, he did with all his heart; and he prospered."

Hezekiah undertook every work בַּעֲבוֹדַת בֵּית־הָאֱלֹהִים ('in the service of the house of God'). The phrase בֵּית־הָאֱלֹהִים בַּעֲבוֹדַת is an expanded form of בְּבֵיתִי of 1 Chr 17:14. Although there is some cultic restriction put on the kings of the Davidic dynasty, seen in the case of Uzziah's punishment (2 Chr 26:16-20), Davidic kings carry important works of the temple by appointing temple personnel, providing offerings, repairing the temple, as well as preparing and completing the temple.

Consequently the phrase, וְהַעֲמַדְתִּיהוּ בְּבֵיתִי וּבְמַלְכוּתִי of 1Chr 17:14 is to be interpreted as: 'I shall establish him in the service of the temple of God and in the kingdom of Israel.'

God establishes Solomon as the supervisor of the temple service. If the Levites carry specific jobs of the temple as priests, singers, gatekeepers and treasurers, King Solomon takes a job of supervision of the temple. In this interpretation, the change from בֵּיתְךָ ('Davidic dynasty') of 2 Sam 7:16 to בְּבֵיתִי ('in the temple of God') of 1 Chr 17:14 would not provide any clue for weakening the Davidic royal promise by the influence of the temple and its cultus. On the contrary, the role of Davidic kings

"בְּבֵיתִי in 1 Chr 17:14: Temple or Kingdom?"

reaches to the area of the temple and the importance of the Davidic dynasty is enhanced.

"The Uniqueness of Jesus As the Beauty of Harmony among Us"

Yong-Sun Yang

We are living in the plural society with people who have different languages, faiths and cultures. Diversity seems to be no more a negative obstacle to be overcome or negated, but an affirmative opportunity to be accepted as the grace of God for us to see the new and unexpected beauty of the world we live in. In this multi-cultural, pluralistic world, however, it is also true that there is a tension or confliction between the actual reality we experience and the traditional doctrines we have as Christians. One of those challenges is the issue of the finality of Jesus Christ as the way, the truth and the life. Is Jesus Christ still the only way to God in this postmodern world where it is generally believed there is no absolute truth any more? If so, in what sense? A general approach to it may be from the actual center of uniqueness of Jesus Christ: ecclesiocentric, Christocentric and theocentric. There is another popular approach, which is from the salvific implication of the uniqueness of Jesus Christ: exclusivism, inclusivism and pluralism. Those approaches are useful and convenient in classifying the range of salvation from the perspective of modern Christianity. However, such traditional classifications seem to overlook the tension between the experiential reality we encounter and the theological doctrines we have in this postmodern world. In this essay, therefore, a different approach is taken by paying a close attention to human experience, language and culture as the essential bases for doing theology. This essay argues that the diversity of our world in language, faiths and culture is not a barrier to be removed but an invitation to the remembrance that the grace of God is here and now.

Three Assumptions

The question of this essay starts from the recognition of the tension between the experiential confession and the theological doctrines.[1] To catch the rich meaning of the experiential tension in reality, it is necessary to approach theological terms and doctrines, taking into account their cultural backgrounds. Being a Christian is the human experience that is the dynamic life, constantly changing and moving. Its colors and shapes vivid are not clearly and sufficiently described in a static and dogmatic expression of language. There is always a gap between concrete experience and abstract doctrines as faith is a matter of life and reality in the ever-changing world. Many linguistic and cultural presuppositions are innate in our confessions. The meaning of theological doctrines cannot be completely free from the cultural and linguistic influence. Therefore, the finality of Jesus Christ in relation to its salvific role always needs a new illumination here and now, not because it is problematic but because it is beneficial to enrich our understanding of our faith in this postmodern world.

This essay presupposes three main assumptions regarding reason, language and culture. The first assumption is about the relationship between theology and culture. Doing theology is the

---

[1] Subjective internal experience rather than externals, as a main warrant, is the starting point of this essay. In that sense, this essay is postmodern rather than modern. But it seems to be better to say that there is no clear distinction between modern and postmodern in the sense that postmodern may be a face of modernity. See David Cheetham, 'Postmodern Freedom and Religion' *Theology* (103/ 811) He assumes, as a realist, that truth is not just something self-constructed. But my assumption is that there is no clear distinction between subjectivity and objectivity, which is why I start from experiential reality below, not from metaphysical reality above.

work of humans who exist in their own social and historical context. It cannot be done in a cultural vacuum.[2] Theology is the product of the culture of the time. Different culture leads to different theology. Another assumption is about the relationship between language and theology.[3] Language as a product of culture is not just a tool to be passively used for developing theological ideas and expressions, but it also may affect and is even able to manipulate our theological thinking as well. Different language leads to different theology. The last one is about the relation between reality and reason. There is always a gap between experiential reality and theological reasoning as there is no objective and absolute facts true to everybody without linguistic and cultural limit. These three assumptions are postmodern, because it is assumed that a universal theory based on the unlimited power of objective reason is not possible without linguistic and cultural distortion internalized in our subjectivity. An experiential approach rather than rational meta-narrative is useful to explore the finality of Jesus Christ in a postmodern world.

Experience, Language and Culture as a Theological Womb

Bonhoeffer's central concern with the focal points of Christ's presence and reality is concisely expressed in his saying that the only way to follow Jesus is by living in the world.[4] Christianness is not an other-worldly separation in a distant religious sphere, but a worldly involvement through costly

---

[2] See Graham Ward, 'Theology and Postmodernism', *Theology* Nov/Dec 1997. I agree with his argument that theology must reflect on social-historical context. Postmodern thinking has much to speak out in that context.

[3] Susan B. Thistlethwaite "Christology and Postmodernism" *Interpretation* 49/3 July 1995. She argues that an innate human reason and subjectivity in the modern perspective is instead a product of social force, primarily language in the postmodern perspective.

[4] Stanley J. Grenz & Roger E. Olson, *20th Century Theology*, (Downers Grove: IVP, 1992) pp.147-156

discipleship in community. Even his worldly Christianity, however, seems to be based on a quite exclusive Christology in the sense that God's revelation coming through only in and through Jesus Christ is the heart of his theology. His limited experiential and cultural context seems to make him stay in exclusive Christology without contradiction. His approach is essential in understanding the problems of the modern Christianity in Germany, but does not seem to be enough to understand Jesus' finality and sufficiency as the way, the truth and the life in the postmodern, plural, multi-cultural society. It is true that he also struggles to find out the meaning of the uniqueness of Jesus Christ by asking an important question that who is Jesus for us today. Theology is a struggle to find out an answer to the never-ending question of who we are and what we want, using the linguistic concept of God in our cultural context. Culture is a horizon we stand at to see the theological landscapes of the world. Different horizon opens up different theological landscapes. In the horizon of a postmodern culture[5], how does the finality of Jesus Christ look like for us?

The term 'uniqueness' is often used in theological arguments without clarification. How to clarify the meaning of the term 'uniqueness' largely depends on the context the term is used. The meaning of 'uniqueness' itself may be differently defined in the different contexts. In the postmodern context, the definition of 'uniqueness' is a matter of relativity without losing its own characteristics. In the modern context, however, 'uniqueness' is generally understood in relation with absoluteness rather than

---

[5] There is considerable disagreement concerning what the postmodern is. But main characteristics are the end of metaphysics, the end of history, the end of the subject, the end of the sign, the end of the ontological order by reason, the end of the unintrusive god of theism, etc. Rather than what is, but what it has just now ceased to be is the main attitude in the postmodern world. See, Adams, Daniel J. "Possibilities for Theology in the Postmodern Era" *Asia Journal Of Theology* (10/1, 1996)   Ward, Graham "Theology and Postmodernism" *Theology* (Nov/Dec, 1997) Lowe, Walter "Prospects For A Postmodern Christian Theology: Apocalyptic Without Reserve" Modern Theology (15/1 Jan.1999)

relativity.⁶ A more careful attention therefore needs to be taken to properly use the term of uniqueness. A right question will be then not "Is Jesus unique or not?" but "In what sense, is Jesus unique or not?"

There are many similar concepts such as finality, centrality, oneness, etc. Such terms as 'one', 'final' and 'central' have more dualistic implication than 'unique.'⁷ Finality is such a concept that it is hard to find a middle area between 'final' and 'not final'. Oneness cannot accommodate a possibility of being in harmony with non-oneness. More flexible terms with less linguistic barriers are necessary in approaching the tension between experiential reality and dogmatic expression. If the vulnerability of language as the product of our culture is to be taken into consideration, 'uniqueness' is a more convenient term with which to discuss a dynamic understanding of Christology in a pluralistic world.

As a Christian, we certainly agree that Jesus Christ is unique in God's plan. The term 'uniqueness' however is not clear when it is used in relation with Jesus' salvific role of salvation. The problematic meaning of uniqueness becomes more complicated in the multi-cultural contexts. Does absolute uniqueness means that there is no salvation outside church or Christianity? Does constitutive uniqueness means that there is a possibility of salvation through Jesus Christ outside church or Christianity? The former is an absolute uniqueness, while the latter is a rather relative one. Both of them are however constitutive not normative, because Jesus Christ is constitutive of salvation in the sense that without Jesus Christ, there is no salvation. Jesus Christ however can be still unique even in the normative Christology. Then, we may ask another question. Is there any ontological reason

---

[6] For example, a postmodernist still can argue that Jesus is unique in his postmodern context. The meaning of uniqueness has different definition in a postmodern world-view. It is possible that the right sort of postmodernism help us to think the meaning of uniqueness. See Walter Lowe, 'Prospects for a postmodern Christian theology: Apocalyptic without reserve', *Modern Theology* 15:1 Jan. 1999.

[7] 'Not final', 'not one' and 'not central' sound like quite strongly quantitative.

for Jesus Christ to be normative or representative[8] to be unique at all? This question is especially relevant and important in a postmodern world where the modern presupposition that there are the absolute norms or facts to be accepted by everybody is no more taken granted.

Different cultural and linguistic backgrounds help to notice the gap between reality itself and language as an expression. The tendency of identification of linguistic expression with reality seems to be quite strong in our modern world. Interestingly, in some Asian languages including Korean and Japanese, it is possible and sometimes more natural to say and write a sentence without a subject, especially 'I'. It is general to use a sentence without subjects. In English, however, the sentences without subjects are not accepted. This is not just a linguistic difference, but it is also implies that there is a cultural issue. The sentence without the subject 'I' is natural in Korean, but strange in English, for example. There are many rooms between 'I' and 'non-I' in Korean culture. A communal concept of 'we' is more frequently used than an individual concept 'I" in many expressions, which may confuse those who have no knowledge in Asian cultural backgrounds imbedded in expressions such as 'our wife', 'our husband', 'our house', to name a few.

This linguistic and cultural difference is however not an impediment. It is a cultural horizon on which we may see the various dimensions of reality in general, and theological landscape in particular. The term 'I' used in Jesus' sayings about his identity

---

[8] Schubert M. Ogden argues that the non-absoluteness of Christianity is not to be the matter of constitutive uniqueness, but representative uniqueness. For him, Hick's pluralism is too much simplifying the differences of religions. The point is not the matter of inclusivism or pluralism but the matter of constitutive or representative. He suggests 'representative' uniqueness as a solution beyond the usual options such as Hick's pluralism, to evade the negative meaning of exclusivism without losing Christian identity. See Schubert M. Ogden *Doing Theology Today*, (Valley Forge, Trinity Press) pp.154-184.

in the Bible[9] does not necessarily mean an exclusive 'I' that negates any other possibility of 'non-I'. The strong identification of Jesus with the Christ might be closely related to the pride and prejudice of modern Christianity. These linguistic and cultural contexts are not the reasons of conflictions but have a possibility of opening up a new perspective with which we may explore the beauty of the theological world shown in the uniqueness of Jesus Christ.

Exclusivism[10]

One of the favorite approaches to the finality of Jesus' salvific role is exclusivism. There is a group of arguments saying that there is no other way to God except Jesus Christ so that other religions are excluded from salvation. Jesus Christ is the one and only way to God. In that sense, Jesus Christ is absolutely unique and constitutive of salvation. Christianity is the only true religion and other religions are wrong. The meaning of uniqueness of Jesus Christ is absolutely exclusive in the sense that other religions are completely excluded from the possibility of salvation. The uniqueness of this exclusive Christology is absolute rather than relative. But, the problems with exclusive Christology can be discussed in many different ways. The basic problem of the exclusive Christology is related to a tension between particularity and universality. In this traditional approach, exclusivism might easily engage in aggressive self-defense in a strong identification

---

[9] See the essay of Seiichi Yagi with a title '"I" in the words of Jesus' in the book; John Hick & Paul Knitter ed. *Myth of Christian Uniqueness:Toward a Pluralistic Theology of Religion.* Maryknoll, NY: Orbis books, 1987.

[10] There are many different arguments in exclusivism. Sometimes, it is difficult to say whether an argument is to belong to exclusivism. I summarize the common points regarded as exclusivism, concentrating on adjectives and nouns used in the exclusive argument.

of Jesus-glory with self-glory.[11] Culturally speaking, it is much fare to say that to have religion is not a matter of God's election but a matter of human fate. Non-Christians who live at the different time and in the different place have no choice but to have their own religion. If non-Christians are excluded just because of being born in the wrong place,[12] God's love should be particular rather than universal, which is against Christian central message about universality of God's love. Linguistically speaking, the exclusive understanding of the meaning of uniqueness of Christ seems to be partly caused by the exclusive way of understanding of 'I' language in Jesus' sayings in the Bible. It is important to take into account the cultural background of language in the different contexts as our language is culturally baptized in a particular time at a particular place.[13]

Inclusivism[14]

There is an argument trying to soften the tension between particularity and universality. Some believe that there may be other ways by general revelations to God even though Christianity is the only true religion by special revelation through Jesus Christ. General revelation is given to other religions so that they may be ways to God. But as far as salvation is concerned, Jesus Christ is the one and only way to God. Non-Christians can be saved not because their ways are correct way to salvation, but because Jesus Christ is the one and only way to salvation. Non-Christians also

---

[11] This point is from both John Hick and Raimundo Panikkar. The tendency of wrong identification in Christian history is quite strongly criticized in Raimundo Panikkar's typology

[12] Geography is an important issue but neglected in the traditional theology. Raimundo Panikkar's geo-theological approach is quite creative and important.

[13] This is one of main arguments of Hick. Panikkar goes further than Hick.

[14] There are many different kinds of inclusivism, for example, pluralistic inclusivism, inclusive pluralism, etc. I just summarize main characteristics.

can be included in salvation through universality of Jesus Christ. In this argument, Jesus Christ is the unique door through where people are included rather than excluded. The meaning of uniqueness in the inclusive Christology still absolute in the sense that Jesus Christ is constitutive of salvation. This inclusive Christology is criticized as a disguised exclusivism. Pluralistic inclusivism is an example of trying to find a solution to the limit of the inclusivism expressed by the slogan that outside Jesus Christ, there is no salvation. Inclusivists continue to maintain that Christianity alone can be the formally true religion, since it alone is the religion established in the unique saving event of Jesus Christ while other religions are fragmentary and inadequate. Non-Christians are anonymously and unknowingly saved through the means of their religions even though Christians are related to the same salvation explicitly and knowingly through the mission of the visible church. This kind of inclusive uniqueness still is open to the same criticism as shown in exclusive Christology. The possibility of getting enriched by the claims and perspectives of other faith-affirmations are very low in this inclusive uniqueness of Jesus Christ. It is not easy to get out of criticism that the tendency of identification of Jesus-glory and self-glory still exists in this inclusivism. Therefore, this approach is not sufficient to see the beauty of the finality of Jesus' salvific role in a postmodern world.

Pluralism[15]

This approach believes that there are plural ways to God. Christianity is not the only way but one of many true ways to God. Christianity is one of many religions, some or all of which may be

---

[15] Pluralism is a very ambiguous term. It seems to be problematic to compare pluralism on a same logical line with exclusivism and inclusivism, because quite different elements and presuppositions are introduced into this paradigm. We do not have to presuppose that pluralism negates uniqueness of Jesus Christ. Pluralists try to see others not from above but from below or same level.

"The Uniqueness of Jesus"

as true as Christianity not only in revelation and but also in salvation. The center of tenets is God rather than Jesus Christ. According to Hick,[16] pluralism is the kind of theological position from which the Christian tradition is seen as one of a plurality of contexts of salvation, within which the transformation of human existence from self-centredness to God or Reality-centredness is occurring.

For pluralists, Christianity is not the one and only way of salvation but one among several, one of the world faiths through which human beings can be savingly related to that ultimate Reality that Christian knows as the heavenly Father. In Hick's understanding, as Schubert M. Ogden points out clearly,[17] pluralism entails asserting not only that there can be several ways of salvation, of which Christianity is but one, but also that there actually are these several ways. Criticism against pluralism is mainly from exclusive and inclusive perspectives. The problems with this plural approach come from its argument that there are true religions or ways of salvation. But, how do we know that there are many true religions without standing on a particular religion? A danger of homogenization shown in exclusivism is also in pluralism.[18] The fruits of religious faith in human life may be the answer of how to know that other religions are true or not. But, in reality, we cannot be independent enough to see things as they are. We cannot get out of our own particular perspectives from which we experience and judge. Universality without particularity has a danger of falling into another exclusive approach in the sense that pluralism has a tendency of excluding the particularity of religions.

---

[16] John Hick "The Non-Absoluteness of Christianity" in John Hick and Paul Knitter ed. *Myth of Christian Uniqueness:Toward a Pluralistic Theology of Religion.* (Maryknoll, Orbis Books, 1996)

[17] See Schubert M. Ogden Doing Theology Today, (Valley Forge, Trinity Press) p.179 He argues for representative uniqueness rather than constitutive uniqueness as a solution beyond the usual options.

[18] See J.A. DiNoia, "Varieties of Religious Aims: Beyond Exclusivism, Inclusivism and Pluralism" p.48 He argues that pluralism tends to homogenize cross-religious variations in doctrines of salvation in the direction of an indeterminate goal.

Pluralism is not only a postmodern approach in the sense of accepting the equal legitimacy of different cultures and incompatible languages, but also a modern one in the sense of positing a Universal reality behind the various particulars. [19] Pluralism is criticized as negating a possibility of genuinely conflicting truth-claims, by stressing a dialogue free of superiority and chauvinism of exclusivism and inclusivism. The confessional and proclamatory elements of dialogue are neglected in pluralism. For example, John B. Cobb, Jr. argues[20] for a Christian superiority in the sense that a tradition having Jesus as the center has in principle no need for exclusive boundaries. Such tradition can be open to transformation by what it learns from others so that, he argues, it can move forward to become a community of faith that is informed by the whole of human history. John B. Cobb, Jr. criticizes pluralism, saying that Christianity, its role in history, its response to pluralistic situation, its potential for becoming more inclusive, is unique like all traditions.[21]

In sum, arguments regarding the uniqueness of Jesus Christ have been divided into the typology having three categories; exclusivism, inclusivism, and pluralism. This typology helps us to compare different meanings of uniqueness of Jesus in relation with salvation. This typology however may create an illusion that proponents of the same category have the same opinion, whereas they actually do not.[22] This is a major intrinsic flaw, misleading people to oversimplify the tension between experiential reality and doctrinal statement. Belonging to the same categories does not necessarily mean the same arguments for the uniqueness of Jesus'

---

[19] See David Cheetham 'Postmodern freedom religion' *Theology* Jan/Feb, 2000
[20] See John B. Cobb, Jr. "Beyond Pluralism" in D' Costa, Gavin *Christian Uniqueness Reconsidered* (New York, Orbis,1990)
[21] Ibid. p.94
[22] See Terrence Tilley 'Christianity and the world religion, a recent Vatican document' *Theological Studies* 60 (1999) He criticizes postmodern freedom from the perspective of a realist.

salvific role.[23] For example, Karl Barth's Christology may be classified into exclusivism because of his absolute, constitutive Christology, and can also be classified into inclusivism because of his universal Christology. This is a general problem of a typology rather than this one only. Another problem is that the concept of salvation itself has quite different range of meanings, which is not taken into consideration in the typology. The meaning of uniqueness of Jesus Christ is not just a matter of salvation, whatever salvation means.[24] Rather, it is a cumulative, dynamic, multi-dimensional, qualitative relationship between Jesus Christ and Christians, non-Christians as well. Rather than rejecting others as imperialistic inclusivist or indifferent pluralist, it is necessary to recognize the changing meaning of uniqueness of Jesus Christ in the context in which those arguments developed. At this stage, John Hick's religio-cultural approach may be helpful to clarify the meaning of uniqueness of Jesus Christ in a postmodern world.

Hick's Religious and Cultural Approach to Uniqueness[25]

John Hick's Christology starts from both an experiential fact that Christianity is one of many religions among several great contexts of salvation, and a theoretical assumption that there is a difference between noumenon and phenomena. He tries to approach to Christology from experiential and historical facts rather than from theoretical statements. For him, religious knowledge is ultimately the fruit of the human quest to understand

---

[23] For example, the concept of uniqueness is misleading if used without clarification. Important question is not whether Jesus Christ is unique or not but in what sense he is unique and why?

[24] See S.Mark Heim 'Salvations: A more pluralistic hypothesis', *Modern theology* 10:4 Oct 1994 He argues pluralism is not religiously pluralistic at all because one religious end is a crucial constitutive element of those arguments. Rather than many gods and one salvation, he suggests many ends or salvations.

[25] Stephen Davis et all ed. *Encountering Jesus*, (Atlanta, John Knox Press, 1988) pp.5-22

reality. Phenomenologically, for him, the Christ is only one of a number of authentic manifestation of the divine reality, the Real as noumenon. The Christianized ambiguous term 'God' is no more helpful for him to approach Christology from historical and experiential facts, because the strictly orthodox terms Christocentrism is already theocentric, since Christ is identified as God. Rather than the ambiguous theocentrism, his choice is to speak not of God but of the Real. In order to affirm the basic authenticity of the different forms of religious experience, theistic and non-theistic, he need to postulate an ultimate reality, which is differently experienced through different cultural backgrounds.

From Hick's point of view, historically speaking, the God-manhood of Jesus with his divine and human natures is rather a humanly constructed theory, than an observed fact in the sense that there are no much historical facts to support the incarnation. The exclusive Chalcedonian definition is no more divinely revelation for him but is a human formulation causing the side effects of traditional Christianity such as colonialism, anti-Semitism and the burning of heretics. The inspiration and grace as a reality in our understanding of Jesus does not require theoretical constructions such as the concepts of the Logos or of the trinity. In his approach, a Christology based on human experience rather than on human speculation is more helpful in the diversity of apparent revelation. He argues that a paradigm shift from Jesus-centered or God-centered to Reality-centered model of the universe of faith is inevitable. The meaning of uniqueness of Jesus Christ is for him no more a matter of incarnation or two nature Christology, rather a matter of transformation from self-centeredness to Reality-centeredness. He tries to overcome the tension between experiential reality and traditional doctrines by removing the Christian self-identification with Jesus and God and opening up a new horizon of the ultimate reality.

In his religious and cultural approach, Jesus Christ is unique not because he is constitutive or normative for others but because he is wholly God in the sense that his agape is the true agape of God at work on earth. His basic assumption regarding noumenon and phenomena does not allow him to accept the meaning of Jesus' uniqueness as the whole of God. Jesus is unique in the sense that God is truly to be encountered in Jesus. Jesus is unique in the sense that Jesus is the center and norm for lives of Christians, without having to insist that he be so for all other human beings. Jesus is unique in the sense that Jesus is the one who is utterly expressive of God not the exhaustive revelation of God. In his Christology, Hick might say that Jesus is still unique.[26]

To sum up, humans live in a specific time and place. Culture is an essential term to understand an identity of being a human living in time and place. Hick's experiential approach choosing culture as an essential element helps to explore the meaning of uniqueness of Jesus Christ from a religio-cultural perspective.

Panikkar's Geographical Approach to Uniqueness[27]

The dilemma between the uniqueness of Jesus and universality of God's love needs a new paradigm. Panikkar introduces geography as one of main coordinates measuring the meaning of the uniqueness of Jesus Christ. He argues that the christic principle is neither a particular event nor a universal religion.[28] Christology is not to be purely deductive but rather empirical and historical because a religion is not a static construct. In his paradigm, the meaning of uniqueness of Jesus Christ moves into different dimension. He assumes that Christology is a product

---

[26] I want to call this uniqueness as a planar uniqueness. His understanding of the meaning of uniqueness is mainly from his religio-cultural approach. Scott Cowdell's typology is a linear uniqueness without consideration of culture

[27] His Christology is mainly from his article. See Raimundo Panikkar, 'The Jordan, The Tiber, and The Ganges', in John Hick& Paul Knitter ed. *Myth of Christian Uniqueness: Toward a Pluralistic Theology of religion*, (Maryknoll, Orbis Books, 1987)

[28] Ibid. p.90

of dynamic relationship among history, culture and geography. To support the argument, he divides the self-understanding of Christians throughout history into five historical periods, pointing out that each of them is still permeating the others. The changing meaning of uniqueness of Jesus Christ is clearly shown in his dynamic geo-theological and historical approach.

Before discussing his meaning of uniqueness of Jesus Christ, it is necessary to clarify the main terms he frequently uses in his arguments regarding Christology. He seems to prefer 'concrete' to 'particular', and 'universal' to 'general.' He argues that the concrete can be universal, not so the particular, in the sense that the concrete is the part for the whole while the particular is the part in the whole.[29] In other words, we may sacrifice the particular for the sake of the whole, but we cannot do that with the concrete. In his way of thinking, universal is not necessarily a quantitative notion. He asks us to change the very perspective of the question. Understanding the uniqueness of Jesus Christ, he points out, we should not confuse the individuality of Christ with our individuation of him; his identity is not his individuation.[30] For example, Christ is unique as any loved child is unique for its parents. Christians stick to their Christ and become exclusive, or they give up their claims, dilute their beliefs, and become at best inclusive, both of the attitudes are equally unacceptable in his Christology. He tries to solve the dilemma by shifting the center from linear history to his theanthropocosmic vision (the divine-human-cosmic), a kind of Trinitarian notion, not of the godhead alone, but of reality including human beings.[31]

His definition of pluralism is not to be confused with plurality. His term of pluralism is not a reduction of plurality to unity, not unity as indispensable ideal, not the truth as one or many,

---

[29] Ibid. p. 107

[30] Individuation may be a product of self-centeredness. John Hick's argument of reality-centeredness seems to be similar to this.

[31] His theanthropocosmic vision is quite interesting in the sense that humans are treated as one of main cores. Humans are not any more just objects of God's salvation. Rather humans are one of the main polars.

not dualistic, not a universal system, not a mere symbol, not denial of the logos, but being aware of our own contingency, limitation, nontransparency of reality.[32] From a modern perspective, his pluralism seems to be strongly postmodern, as he argues that Christian pluralistic attitudes should be not single Christian self-understanding, not supersystem, not one single perspective of what the other Christian views should be. According to his understanding of pluralism, the argument of many saviors in the world is a non-pluralistic assertion,[33] because a pluralistic Christology begins by denying the meaningfulness of any quantitative individualization. For him, Christian self-understanding is a function of the all-embracing myth reigning at a particular time and place.

Therefore, according to his geographical approach, the statement "Jesus is Christ" is not identical to the statement "Christ is Jesus." That may be his short answer to the question of the meaning of uniqueness of Jesus Christ. Jesus is simply one concrete historical name for the Christ, which can also be called, by other historical name.[34] In other words, we should not identify the christic fact of Christianness with Christianity or Christendom, because there is no need for one single view of Christ. No single notion can comprehend the reality of Christ. Religions may be incommensurable with each other. Each religion is unique with the uniqueness of every real being. He argues that we should accept the emergence of a new Christian consciousness tied neither to Christian (Western) civilization, nor to Christian (institutionalized) religion. Some may even shun the name "Christian" because the "Christian" label may be understood as a mere continuation of the

---

[32] Ibid. pp.109-110

[33] Pluralism is generally understood as accepting many saviors. But he denies this misunderstanding as quantitative.

[34] Joseph Wong, "Anonymous Christians: Karl Rahner's Pneuma-Christocentrism and an East-West Dialogue" *Theological Studies* (55/4, 1994) He argues that Panikkar's universal Christology of a Christ disconnected with the historical Jesus creates serious problems. But this problematic argument of Panikkar is to be understood in his cultural and geographical paradigm.

past. To be a Christian, he argues, is difficult because it requires the personal discipline, the courage to face not only the profane world, but also the ecclesiastical institutions. His conclusion is that the meaning of the uniqueness of Jesus Christ is to be understood nor normatively neither in representatively but in a sort of mystical experience.

Problems with Panikkar's arguments are however related to a very Indian concept of God and religion. Geographical Ganges does not fully represent the many faces of different faiths. For example, Karl Barth's exclusive position denying of Christian faiths as a religion also would have many things to say against Panikkar's dialogical Christology. However, Panikkar's unknown Christ in his culture and geography is quite unique in understanding the meaning of uniqueness of Jesus Christ in a postmodern world. Barth seems to try to solve the meaning of uniqueness of Jesus Christ without falling into a religion, by putting his Christology above culture, geography and reason. But, reality is not such a thing as to be completely explained out in a universal dogma or metanarrative. Humans are limited beings not only in the sense that power of human reason is limited but also in the sense that humans live in a specific time and place. However, the limit is again a possibility in a postmodern world. The difference is not an impediment but a spectacle with which to see the beauty of the unexpected world. The uniqueness of Jesus Christ is an enriching conceptual tool with which we may explore the true relationship among God, the world, and man in general, and 'you' and 'I' as 'we' in particular.

Uniqueness as Openness Rather than a Closure

The meaning of uniqueness of Jesus Christ has so many colors and faces, changing in time and places. Any single Christology or creedal formula is not enough to catch the enriching concept of the uniqueness of Jesus in the postmodern world. In addition to the changing colors and shapes, an inevitable subjective experience in particular culture and language makes it much complicated to see a reality as it is. However, we cannot see anything unless we stand on a particular position as a vantage point. That is a dilemma of human existence. Because of this tension between ever-changing experiential reality and traditional dogma, this essay approaches the uniqueness of Jesus Christ from concrete experience rather than from universal theory.

In this context, a linguistic and cultural approach gives many useful tools with which to explore the difficulty of seeing the true meaning of the uniqueness of Jesus Christ in a postmodern world. It is argued that the term 'difference' may be a much better concept than 'finality' or 'oneness' to understand the uniqueness of Jesus in the postmodern society. Even though we cannot deny that language is a necessary, useful and even inevitable, it does not always describe a multi-dimensional reality without cultural distortions. If we accept such a postmodern presupposition, a linguistic and cultural approach is quite useful to see reality as it is without misunderstanding and prejudice.

The term of uniqueness of Jesus Christ is not such a word given to us objectively, independently outside time and place, but a word we build up in our tradition of culture in particular time and place. Three theologians' typologies are discussed to see how they digest and theorize the dilemma caused by the tension between the Jesus of history and the Christ of faith. I tried to show that modern typology is not only unable to solve the dilemma clearly, but also may mislead the meaning of uniqueness of Jesus Christ.

Therefore, a postmodern approach is chosen to see the structure of dilemma by deconstructing the meaning of uniqueness of Jesus Christ. Jesus is unique not necessarily in the modern sense that the uniqueness of Jesus is to be applied and extended to every other religion as the absolute way or best norm, but possibly in the postmodern sense that different time and place give rise to different Christologies. Truth needs to be deabsolutized to see the truth itself. Christianness is probably a better linguistic expression representing the true identity of being a Christian in a postmodern world than Christianity as institutions or Christendom as civilization.

The meaning of uniqueness is to found in a cumulative approach, rather than Christology alone. Identification of oneself with Jesus Christ caused by self-defense might be a byproduct of modernity that defies the diversity of human existence. Postmodern Christianness does not exclude anyone in the name of Jesus Christ who excludes no body. Rather than what is, but what it has just now ceased to be has much to speak out for the uniqueness of Jesus Christ. In that sense, Jesus Christ is still unique in a postmodern world.

The ever-changing reality of the world is always beyond our limited ability to see, feel, and talk about. That is however not frustration but hope as the uniqueness of Jesus Christ is meaningful even in a postmodern world. The story of a prodigal son and his brother in the parable of the lost son shows two different faces of our salvation: experiential confession and theological dogma (Lk 15: 11-32). The uniqueness of Jesus in this postmodern world is probably not in our proud confession that we have served and obeyed through our whole life, but probably in our humble recognition and constant remembrance that the Father was, is and will be with us, and everything God has is ours. The uniqueness of Jesus Christ is a window through which we may see the beauty of the multi-faceted grace of God hidden in the postmodern world here and now.

Bibliography

Adams, Daniel J. "Possibilities for Theology in the Postmodern Era", *Asia Journal of Theology,* (10/1, 1996)

Aleaz, K.P. "Pluralistic Inclusivism", *Asia Journal of Theology,* (12/2, Oct. 1998)

Cheetham, David. "Postmodern Freedom and Religion", *Theology,* (103/811, 2000)

Cowell, Scott. *Is Jesus Unique?* (Mahwah: Paulist Press, 1996)

Davis, Stephen T. et all ed. *Encountering Jesus,* (Atlanta: John Knox Press, 1988)

D'Costa, Gavin. *Christian Uniqueness Reconsidered,* (New York: Orbis, 1990)

Grenz, Stanley J. & Olson, Roger E. *20th Century theology- God & the World in a Transitional Age*, (Downers Grove: IVP, 1992)

Heim, S. Mark. "Salvations: A More Pluralistic Hypothesis", *Modern Theology* (10/4, 1994)

Hick, John. *The Rainbow of Faith,* (London: SCM Press, 1995)

------------- "Is Christianity the Only True Religion", *Theology,* (Sep/Oct, 1998)

Hick, John and Paul Knitter ed. *Myth of Christian Uniqueness: Toward a Pluralistic Theology of Religion,* (Maryknoll: Orbis Books, 1987)

Knitter, Paul F. *No Other Name?* (Maryknoll: Orbis Books, 1985)

Lowe, Walter. "Prospects For A Postmodern Christian Theology: Apocalyptic Without Reserve", *Modern Theology,* (15/1, Jan. 1999)

Merrigan, Terrence. "Religious Knowledge In The Pluralist theology of Religions", *Theological Studies,* (58, 1997)

Ogden, Schubert M. *Doing Theology Today,* (Valley Forge: Trinity Press)

Panikkar, Raimundo. *The Unknown Christ of Hinduism* (Maryknoll: Orbis, 1981)

------------------------. "The Jordan, The Tiber, and The Ganges - three kairological moments of Christic self-consciousness" in Hick, John & Paul Knitter ed. *Myth of Christian Uniqueness: Toward a Pluralistic Theology of Religion* (Maryknoll: Orbis books, 1987) pp.89-116

Thistlethwaite, Susan Brooks. "Christology and Postmodernism: Not Everyone Who Says to Me 'Lord, Lord ", *Interpretation,* (49/3, 1995)

Tilley, Terrence W. "Christianity and The World Religions, A Recent Vatican document", *Theological Studies,* (60/2. 1999)

Ward, Graham. "Theology and Postmodernism", *Theology,* (Nov/Dec, 1997)

Wong, Joseph H. "Anonymous Christians: Karl Rahner's Pneuma-Christocentrism and An East-West Dialogue", *Theological Studies,* (55/4, Dec. 1994)

"Intertextual Time Capsule of Luke 4:16-30:
The Import of Luke's Two Significant Intertextual
Additions for Understanding the Lukan Agenda"[1]

Heerak Christian Kim

Luke 4:16-30 – often referred to as "Jesus' Preaching in Nazareth" – is thought to be central to understanding the writings of Luke. Its import for the Gospel tradition is evident in its attestation in other synoptic gospels (Matthew 13:53-58 and Mark 6:1-6a). What is significant in Luke's pericope are the two Lukan additions; namely, Luke 4:17-21 and Luke 4:25-27. I would argue that these two additions shed invaluable light on Lukan theology and the use of the Old Testament in Luke. Luke 4:17-21 contains a quotation of Isaiah 61:1-2 and Isaiah 58:6. Morna D. Hooker writes: "The quotation follows that LXX of Isaiah 61, but omits one phrase ('to heal the broken-hearted") and includes another ('to set at liberty those who are oppressed') taken from Isa. 58.6; this minor variation is probably of no great significance" ("Beginning with Moses and from all the Prophets," *Jesus to John: Essays on Jesus and New Testament Christology in Honour of Marinus de Jonge*, edited by Martinus C. De Boer. [Sheffield: Sheffield Academic Press, 1993, pp. 216-230], p. 222). I would argue that the variation is, in fact, very significant and that it points out the intertextual relationship between Luke and the Hebrew Bible.[2]

---

[1] This academic paper was delivered at the 2006 Society of Biblical Literature Annual Meeting in Washington, DC, at the Scripture in Early Judaism and Christianity section.

[2] More often than not scholars have focused on the question of messianic (or prophetic) role (or office) of Jesus of Nazareth (Bart J. Koet, "Isaiah in Luke-Acts," *Isaiah in the New Testament*, eds. Steve Moyise and Maarten J. J.

The addition betrays the perspective of a post-70 Christian interpretation of the antecedent Hebrew Bible.[3] This intertextual *Tendenz* in Luke is confirmed in the second large addition in the Luke 4:16-30 pericope. Luke 4:25-27 does not contain a direct quote. However, it contains a strategic explication of antecedent Hebrew Bible traditions of Elijah and Elisha. This Lukan addition illustrates again a post-70 Christian interest [4] in the use of antecedent Hebrew Bible texts. Containing both the use of quotes and the paraphrase of Hebrew Bible antecedent texts, Luke 4:16-30 opens the door to understanding intertextuality in Luke and

---

Menken [London: T & T Clark International, 2005, pp. 79-100], p. 84). See also E. J. Tinsley, *The Gospel according to Luke* (Cambridge: At the University Press, 1965), p. 54; also, François Bovon, *Das Evangelium nach Lukas* (Zürich: Benziger Verlag, 1989), p. 212. But it is now time to think critically about the alteration in terms of Jewish identity, both individual and nationalistic, in light of stated Gentile mission, which the pericope is clearly concerned with. This is the significant contribution of my research.

[3] Klyne Snodgrass' comments cannot be dismissed. Snodgrass writes that Early Christians "used the Old Testament to prove their Christian theology and to solve Christian problems" (Klyne Snodgrass, "The Use of the Old Testament in the New," *Interpreting the NewTestament: Essays on Method and Issues*, eds. David Alan Black & David S. Dockery [Nashville: Broadman & Holman Publishers, 2001, pp. 209-229], p. 209). Thus, Snodgrass concludes: "No subject is perhaps more important for the understanding of the Christian faith than the use of the Old Testament in the New Testament" (p. 209).

[4] Barnabas Lindars states that using Isaiah to argue for Gentile mission was a distinctive trait of Paul. In light of this, Lindars speculates: "It should be seriously considered whether this is not due to the influence of St. Paul in placing the preaching to the Gentiles at the very centre of the proclamation of salvation" (Barnabas Lindars, *New Testament Apologetic: The Doctrinal Significance of the Old Testament Quotations* {London: SCM Press Ltd, 1961}, p. 248). Lindars' speculation that the Lukan emphasis on Gentile mission is evidence of Paul's influence may have some merit. However, I would argue that the influence is more directly related to original Jesus tradtions. This is clear in Jesus traditions that are academically and almost universally accepted as belonging to the ministry of Jesus of Nazareth himself. Open Table Fellowship clearly shows that Jesus of Nazareth characterized his missions with those whom Judaism disenfranchised and othered. Also, Jesus of Nazareth's frequent contact with and ministry to the ritually impure may have been considered by many religious Jews as worse than close contacts with Gentiles.

provides a window view into the direction of New Testament intertextuality.

The reason why the omission of "to heal the broken-hearted" and the addition of "to set at liberaty those who are oppressed" is significant is that it sheds light on Lukan theology and the use of the Old Testament in Luke.[5] In a sense, therefore, the quote of Isaiah in Luke 4:17-21 sets the tone for the whole pericope. The later reference to the Old Testament found in Luke 4:25-27 follows the thematic tone set earlier.[6] I would actually argue that the omission not only sets the tone for this pericope in the Gospel of Luke but for the whole Gospel of Luke.[7] In a sense, it can be seen as a type of "displaced thesis sentence" or an encapsulated thematic statement for Luke. How would this be the case?

---

[5] William Hendricksen correctly identifies that Jesus excerpted the portions of the Prophets needed for his preaching, but does not link what the significance of the connection is (William Hendriksen, *Exposition of the Gospel according to Luke* [Grand Rapids: Baker Book House, 1978], p. 253).

[6] Snodgrass makes an important comment that Jesus of Nazareth and the Early Christians adapted Old Testament texts in the context of the traditional ways those texts were interpreted in the Judaism of the time (Snodgrass, "The Use of the Old Testament in the New," pp. 216-217). He is mostly correct. His error is in not emphasizing strongly enough that Jesus of Nazareth subverted the traditional Jewish interpretation, which is the case here. For a good example of this, read my book, *Key Signifier as Literary Device*, particularly the chapter on how the Book of Esther was "adapted" for the Christian audience in light of the dominant understanding of that text within the Judaism of Jesus of Nazareth's time.

[7] David Aune argues that the function of Luke must be seen in light of its own stated purpose in Luke 1:4. Aune writes: "He wants to provide his patron with 'exact information' (*asphaleia*) about the historical and theological basis for the Christian faith" (David E. Aune, *The New Testament in Its Literary Environment* [Philadelphia: The Westminster Press, 1987], p. 136). The omission should be examined in light of this function of Luke. In this regard, John Reuman's comments are helpful. Reumann writes regarding the Gospel of Luke: "It is above all the gospel that connects Jesus with the church that resulted, and with the Spirit as the vehicle for the next stage of God's ongoing salvific activity" (John Reumann, *Variety and Unity in New Testament Thought* [Oxford: Oxford University Press, 1991], p. 63).

To answer this question, we must first ask why did Luke, or the author of the Gospel of Luke, omit the statement "to heal the broken-hearted"?[8] The response is quite simple, really. The Gospel of Luke is not interested in portraying Jesus of Nazareth as healing the broken-hearted. He is not described as one who is trying to assuage the despondency of his audience. In fact, Jesus of Nazareth is described as confrontational and acerbic in sensitive situations even where the broken-hearted are involved. This is certainly the case in the Luke 4:16-30 pericope.

Jesus of Nazareth's acerbic attitude toward the broken-hearted is clearly visible in his rant which contains the Old Testament reference in Luke 4:25-27. He prefaces the rant with a statement that no prophet is accepted in his hometown. Apparently, he perceived his audience, those from his hometown of Nazareth, as rejecting him. They had questioned his identity by asking about his identity as Joseph's son. But there really was no reason for Jesus of Nazareth to become sensitive about this question. The fact is that the Jews in the synagogue in Nazareth are not indicated as having rejected Jesus of Nazareth, yet. In fact, all the other Gospel attestations show this to be true.

And Luke 4:23 shows that it is Jesus of Nazareth himself who assumes that the Jews of Nazareth were rejecting him by asking that question. Clearly, this assumption is to be seen as misguided for the simple fact that most prophets in the Old Testament are described in terms of their parents. Isaiah 1:1 clearly describes Isaiah as son of Amos. Jeremiah 1:1 describes Jeremiah as the son of Hilkiah. It was normative in the Hebrew

---

[8] Joseph A. Fitzmyer, S.J. argues that Luke faithfully preserved the primitive kerygma of Jesus of Nazareth while giving it "a distinctive Lucan nuance" (Joseph A. Fitzmyer, S.J., *To Advance the Gospel: New Testament Studies* [Grand Rapids: William B. Eerdmans Publishing Company, 1981], p. 252). C. H. Dodd and Barnabas Lindars both agree that Jesus of Nazareth is the originator of the exegetical methodology of the New Testament (vis-à-vis the Old Testament) (D. Moody Smith, Jr., "The Use of the Old Testament in the New," *The Use of the Old Testament in the New and Other Essays: Studies in Honor of William Franklin Stinespring*, ed. James M. Efird [Durham: Duke University Press, 1972, pp. 3-65], p. 23).

Bible tradition to describe God's prophets through their human lineage. Thus, when the Jews of the synagogue in Nazareth asked if Jesus of Nazareth is the son of Joseph, they are not going against the Jewish tradition of identifying a prophet by his father. There was no reason, based on the Hebrew Bible tradition, for Jesus of Nazareth to take offense at the line of questioning that was normative for the Jews of Jesus of Nazareth's time. It was a legitimate question[9] – one that was to identify Jesus in the same way Jeremiah and Isaiah were identified in the Old Testament.

However, Jesus of Nazareth takes offense and goes on a rhetorical rant. It was as if Jesus of Nazareth wanted to disqualify himself from being respected as their prophet. He says to the Jews that they would surely tell him, "Physician, heal thyself." This is an assumption made by Jesus of Nazareth. There is really no indication that the Jews of the synagogue would have taken that line of questioning. Jesus seems to get offended for no apparently good reason.

Not only does Jesus of Nazareth seem to assume too much, he seems to be angry that they may ask him to do miracles in Nazareth that he did in Capernaum. Why should Jesus of Nazareth be offended that the people there want to have their sick healed as the people of Capernaum? Should not Jesus of Nazareth want to heal the broken-hearted? There were surely mothers who were suffering from the illness of their children who were facing death. There were surely those who were broken-hearted because they were crippled from birth or blind from birth and wanted to be healed. Is it not an act of faith to want healing from Jesus of Nazareth, the true representative of God? Why did Jesus of Nazareth take such an aggressive tone? Why did Jesus of Nazareth not want to heal the broken-hearted?

Clearly, the omission of "to heal the broken-hearted" is intentional. Jesus of Nazareth did not want to heal the broken-hearted. If it were included in the quote, the very words of Jesus of

---

[9] Fitzmyer actually believes that the question was "one of pleasant surprise or admiration" (Joseph A. Fitzmyer, S.J., *The Gospel according to Luke (1-IX)* [New York: Doubleday, 1970], p. 535).

Nazareth that the Isaiah passage was fulfilled would be nonsequitor at best and a flat-out lie at worst. Clearly, Jesus of Nazareth did not want to heal in Nazareth. Jesus of Nazareth was not interested in healing the broken-hearted.

This position of Jesus of Nazareth is clear in the Old Testament reference found in Luke 4:25-27. Jesus of Nazareth was rejecting Nazareth, and by extension, his *patris*,[10] and accepting the Gentiles as his people. There are two examples given. One was the example of Elijah during the time there was a famine for three and a half years. Jesus of Nazareth explicitly states that there were a lot of widows suffering in Israel during this time of prophet Elijah. And Jesus of Nazareth is explicit in stating that prophet Elijah refused to go to any of the widows of Israel. Instead, Elijah went to a Gentile woman, a widow from Sidon. Of course, Jesus of Nazareth's idea is clear. Elijah refused to heal the broken-hearted in Israel.

The second example, a reference from the Old Testament, that Jesus of Nazareth's sermon provides in Luke 4:25-27 also clearly shows the idea that the broken-hearted of Israel were refused healing. The second example is that of Elisha the Prophet. Jesus of Nazareth claimed that Elisha refused to heal anyone in Israel with leprosy. The broken-hearted of Israel were refused healing. Instead, Elisha added salt to injury of the broken-hearted in Israel by healing Naaman the Syrian of leprosy. The broken-hearted of Israel were refused healing and their broken-heartedness was exacerbated as Jesus of Nazareth emphasized the healing of a commander in the enemy's army. It would be similar in today's context to saying that there were many in the USA who are suffering from cancer, but God's prophet in the USA did not heal a single person in America suffering from cancer except for Al Queda's Number Two.

---

[10] Fitzmyer does not go far enough when he states that vv. 25-27 provides justification from the OT for the Christian missions to the Gentiles (Fitzmyer, *The Gospel according to Luke (I-IX)*, p. 537). Clearly, Jesus of Nazareth is manipulating the Old Testament to argue that God rejects Israel and accepts the Gentiles, instead.

The response of the Jews of the synagogue in Nazareth is understandable. They took insult from the comments of Jesus of Nazareth who was throwing salt in their broken-hearted wounds, so they wanted to kill him.[11] Jesus of Nazareth's pro-Gentile position and anti-Israel position made the Jews feel greater pain as they keenly felt themselves under the yoke of Roman Rule. Jews were under the authority of the Roman Empire and Jews were looking and hoping for Jewish independence. They did not need a prophet to tell them that God preferred Gentiles to them.

If we are to understand the Jewish audience of Jesus of Nazareth as those who were under the Roman rule, we are compelled to answer a question. How are we to understand the quote, "to set at liberty those who are oppressed"? Were not the Jews oppressed by the Romans? Were not the Jews who needed the freedom? Interestingly enough, Jesus of Nazareth did not describe Jewish subjugation under the Romans as oppression. This is clear in Jesus of Nazareth's command to pay the Roman imperial tax faithfully (Luke 20:25). It is important to remember that tax collectors in Israel were hated and seen even as ritually impure because they collected taxes on behalf of the Roman Empire that was oppressing Israel. While refuting the notion of Roman oppression, Jesus of Nazareth describes Jewish religious leaders as the oppressors.[12] Luke 12:1 gives Jesus of Nazareth's

---

[11] Fitzmyer describes the Jewish rejection of Jesus of Nazareth as "hostile, even diabolic, rejection" (Fitzmyer, *The Gospel according to Luke (I-IX)*, p. 528). Fitzmyer argues that "The rejection of him by the people of his hometown is a miniature of the rejection of him by the people of his own *patris* in the larger sense" (p. 529).

[12] This important point is not even considered by François Bovon, who, much like the rest of the commentators on Luke, operates from the model that the year of Jubilee was extended *first* to Jews (Bovon, *Das Evangelium nach Lukas (Lk 1, 1-9.50)*, p. 215). What is needed is bringing in much of the research in the last 25 years on the radical nature of the Jesus movement (Theissen, Nerey, Holmberg, etc.) that indicates that from the beginning, the Jesus movement was meant to oppose Judaism, whether institutional, mainline, or otherwise. It is my assertion that the Nazareth sermon, often described as Jesus of Nazareth' sermon inaugurating his ministry, clearly identified Jews and the Jewish religion as the oppressors and "jubilee" to be from them.

warnings against the Pharisees. Luke 11:46 clearly shows Jesus of Nazareth claiming that the Pharisees were the oppressors: "And you experts in the law, woe to you, because you load people down with burdens they can hardly carry, and you yourselves will not lift one finger to help them."

Not only are the Jewish religious leaders seen as oppressors of people, they are described as oppressors of God's prophets. In Luke 11:47-49, Jesus of Nazareth claims: "Woe to you, because you build tombs for the prophets, and it was your forefathers who killed them. So you testify that you approve of what your forefathers did; they killed the prophets, and you build their tombs. Because of this, God in his wisdom said, 'I will send them prophets and apostles, some of whom they will kill and others they will persecute." Besides the testimony of Jesus of Nazareth that it is Jewish religious leadership that kills and persecutes true representatives of God, his warnings to his disciples against Jewish religious authorities show that Jesus of Nazareth considered Jewish religion and Jewish religious leaders as the oppressors. In Luke 12:11 Jesus of Nazareth warns his disciples: "When you are brought before synagogues, rulers and authorities, do not worry about how you will defend yourselves or what you will say, for the Holy Spirit will teach you at that time what you should say." Clearly, Jesus of Nazareth portrays Jewish religious leaders and the Jewish religion as the oppressors, and not the Romans or the Roman Empire. Thus, in his quote "to set at liberty those who are oppressed," Jesus of Nazareth was talking about setting free and giving liberty to those who are oppressed by Jewish religious leaders.

The attack of Jewish religious oppression and the push for liberty from that Jewish oppression is clear in Jesus of Nazareth's prophecies of destruction of Jerusalem (Luke 13:34-35).[13] Not

---

[13] Markus J. Borg argues that Jesus of Nazareth was concerned with the renewal of Israel rather than preparing a community for the end (Markus J. Borg, *The Glory of Christ in the New Testament* [Oxford: Clarendon, 1987], pp. 209ff.). Ben Wiebe notes that they do not need to be mutually exclusive (Ben Wiebe, "The Focus of Jesus' Eschatology," *Self-Definition and Self-Discovery in Early*

only does Jesus of Nazareth mention the destruction of Jerusalem, he is quite descriptive. In Luke 21:20, Jesus of Nazareth describes: "When you see Jerusalem being surrounded by armies, you will know that its desolation is near." Jesus of Nazareth further explains that the army will be a Gentile army in Luke 21:24. Thus, with the advent of Gentile armies will the Jewish oppression against followers of Jesus of Nazareth end. The liberty that Jesus of Nazareth is calling for is destruction of Jewish religious leadership and their localized places of worship in Israel. Jewish religious leaders of Jerusalem are the oppressors. The Roman and Gentile invaders of Israel are the liberators. Jesus of Nazareth's sermon in the synagogue of Nazareth was proclaiming the beginning of that process. The word is fulfilled with the coming of Jesus of Nazareth.

Thus, unlike Professor Hooker, I would argue that the omission and the addition are critically important for understanding not only this pericope but the main thrust of Lukan theology. Jesus of Nazareth did not come to heal the broken hearted of Israel. Instead, he had come to set Israel free from the yoke of Jewish religious rule. Israel will be purged of Jewish leadership, and Gentile armies will destroy Israel, fulfilling the prophecy of Jesus of Nazareth to set at liberty those who are oppressed by Jewish religion and Jewish religious leaders.

The post-70 AD Christian community was quite aware of the death of Jesus of Nazareth recorded in the Gospels as the fruit of the collusion and the conspiracy of the Jews. This tradition is repeated throughout the New Testament. Not only did the Jews kill Jesus of Nazareth, they continued to kill the followers of Jesus of Nazareth. In fact, St. Paul, the Apostle of Heart Set Free, was the greatest testimony to the systematic persecution and on-going conspiracy of the Jews against the followers of Christ. St. Paul describes his ways in the ways of the law, commissioned behind

---

Christianity: A Study in Changing Horizons, eds. David J. Hawkins and Tom Robinson [Lewiston: The Edwin Mellen Press, 1990, pp. 121-146], p. 128). I would argue that Jesus of Nazareth was arguing for the end to Israel as a community favored by God.

closed doors by Jewish religious leaders to hunt down, persecute, and even kill followers of Jesus of Nazareth in the name of Judaism. The self-testimony in the Book of Galatians substantiates the historical account in the Book of Acts.

    For this post-70 AD Christian community, their liberty from Judaism and Jewish religious leadership was in significant part due to the fact that God destroyed Jerusalem using Gentile armies and scattered Jewish religious leadership throughout the Diaspora. From their position of weakness, Jews no longer could persecute Christians. Jerusalem had been completely destroyed by the Romans in 70 AD. Jews did not have a homeland or a country to leverage their power against the followers of Jesus of Nazareth. For the post-70 AD Christians who remembered the conspiracy of the Jews in persecuting the followers of Jesus of Nazareth, it was liberty and freedom that came to existence when the Gentiles destroyed Jerusalem and Israel. It is consistent with Lukan theology as well as the understanding of the post-70 AD Christian communities that it was grace of God that God used Gentile armies to completely destroy Jerusalem and Israel. If God did not do this, systematic persecution and effective conspiracy of the Jews against the followers of Jesus of Nazareth would have continued, unabated.

Bibliography

Aune, David E. *The New Testament in Its Literary Environment.* Philadelphia: The Westminster Press, 1987.

Bailey, James L., and Lyle D. Vander Broek, *Literary Forms in the New Testament: A Handbook.* Louisville: Westminster/John Knox Press, 1992.

Black, David Alan, and David S. Dockery. *Interpreting the New Testament: Essays on Methods and Issues.* Nashville: Broadman & Holman Publishers, 2001.

Blount, Brian K. *Cultural Interpretation: Reorienting New Testament Criticism.* Minneapolis: Fortress Press, 1995.

Borg, Marcus J. *The Glory of Christ in the New Testament.* Oxford: Clarendon Press, 1987.

Bovon, François. *Das Evangelium nach Lukas (Lk 1,1-9,50).* Zürich: Benziger Verlag, 1989.

Calvin, John. *Commentary on a Harmony of the Evangelists, Matthew, Mark, and Luke.* Translated by the Rev. William Pringle. Grand Rapids: Baker Book House, 1989.

Fitzmyer, Joseph A., S.J. *The Gospel according to Luke (I-IX).* New York: Doubleday, 1970.

France, R. T. *Jesus and the Old Testament: His Application of Old Testament Passages to Himself and His Mission.* Downers Grove: Inter-Varsity Press, 1971.

Hawkin, Daivd J., and Tom Robinson. *Self-Definition and Self-Discovery in Early Christianity: A Study in Changing Horizons*. Lewiston: The Edwin Mellen Press, 1990.

Hendriksen, William. *Exposition of the Gospel according to Luke*. Grand Rapids: Baker Book House, 1978.

Hester, James D., and J. David Hester (Editors). *Rhetorics and Hermenuetics: Wilhelm Wuellner and His Influence*. New York: T. & T. Clark International, 2004.

Holmgren, Frederick C. *The Old Testament and the Significance of Jesus: Embracing Change – Maintaining Christian Identity*. Grand Rapids: William B. Eerdmans Publishing Company, 1999.

Johnson, Franklin. *The Quotations of the New Testament from the Old Considered in the Light of General Literature*. Philadelphia: American Baptist Publication Society, 1895.

Kaiser, Walter C., Jr. *The Uses of the Old Testament in the New*. Chicago: Moody Press, 1985.

Kim, Heerak Christian. *Key Signifier as Literary Device: Its Definition and Function in Literature and Media*. Lewiston: Edwin Mellen Press, 2006.

Leishman, Thomas Linton. *The Interrelation of the Old and New Testament*. New York: Vantage Press, 1968.

Lindars, Barnabas, S.S.F. *New Testament Apologetic: The Doctrinal Significance of the Old Testament Quotations*. London: SCM Press Ltd., 1961.

Maclaren, Alexander. *Expositions of Holy Scripture (Volume 6): Gospel of St. Mark 9-16, Gospel of St. Luke.* Grand Rapids: Wm. B. Eerdmans Publishing Company, 1959.

Moyise, Steven, and Maarten J. J. Menken (Editors). *Isaiah in the New Testament.* London: T. & T. Clark International, 2005.

Olbricht, Thomas H., and Anders Eriksson (Editors). *Rhetoric, Ethic, and Moral Persuasion in Biblical Discourse: Essays from the 2002 Heidelberg Conference.* New York: T. & T. Clark International, 2005.

Reumann, John. *Variety and Unity in New Testament Thought.* Oxford: Oxford University Press, 1991.

Stöger, Alois. *The Gospel according to St. Luke (Volume 1).* New York: Herder and Herder, 1969.

Tinsley, E. J. *The Gospel according to Luke.* Cambridge: At the University Press, 1965.

Zahn, Theodor. *Das Evangelium des Lucas.* Leipzig: A. Deichert'sche Verlagsbuchhandlung Nachf., 1913.

www.ingramcontent.com/pod-product-compliance
Lightning Source LLC
Chambersburg PA
CBHW031316150426
43191CB00005B/249